The Gospel According to
the Blues

The Gospel According to
the Blues

Gary W. Burnett

CASCADE *Books* · Eugene, Oregon

THE GOSPEL ACCORDING TO THE BLUES

Cascade Books
An Imprint of Wipf and Stock Publishers
199 W. 8th Ave., Suite 3
Eugene, OR 97401

www.wipfandstock.com

ISBN 13: 978-1-62032-725-8

Cataloguing-in-Publication data:

Burnett, Gary W.

    The gospel according to the blues / Gary W. Burnett.

    viii + 162 pp. ; 23 cm. Includes bibliographical references.

    ISBN 13: 978-1-62032-725-8

    1. Blues (Music)—History and criticism. 2. Blues musicians. 3. Christian ethics. I. Title.

ML3521 .B80 2014

Manufactured in the U.S.A.

With thanks to my wonderful
and talented wife, Christine,
for her support and encouragement.
She is my true "kind-hearted woman."

"And here's to the blues, the real blues—
where there's a hint of hope in every cry of desperation."

David Mutti Clark

Contents

one

The Gospel According to the Blues

Introduction

My first introduction to the blues was when I was a teenager. My friend George Lowden (who has since become one of the world's leading acoustic guitar makers) lent me an album entitled *The World of Blues Power*, made in 1969, which was a compilation of stuff by John Mayall's Bluesbreakers with Eric Clapton, Ten Years After, Peter Green, and Savoy Brown.

As a boy brought up in a very conservative church in Northern Ireland, my exposure to music was pretty limited. That is to say—very limited. I knew a lot of hymns and choruses and a bit of classical music from my years of learning piano—but beyond that I was green. The pop revolution of the sixties with The Beatles and The Rolling Stones and so on had largely passed me by—but, given that George was a bit older than me and a pretty cool guy, I borrowed the album, took it home, and put it on the turntable.

When I listened to Clapton playing "All Your Lovin', Pretty Baby" and Savoy Brown singing "taste and try before you buy," not to mention some more rather tasty lyrics later on in that song that certainly were not the sort of things discussed in the church in which I had been brought up—I was hooked on the blues. The next stop was another album George lent me, by Sonny Terry and Brownie McGhee—this time not the electric blues of Eric Clapton and John Mayall, but much more raw, Delta-style blues with acoustic guitar and harmonica.

As I listened, I realized that there was something about this blues music that seemed to reach right inside of me and just grab my innards and twist them. It was something visceral: it felt real, it felt important—in a

1

way that the pop stuff most of my friends were listening to didn't. And that really is the essence of the blues. It's music that goes deep; it moves you; it seems to be able to speak to you in ways that are far from superficial.

And so began a lifelong love of the blues—music from a culture and time far removed from mine, and yet which has had the power to draw me again and again over the years. As time has gone on, I've increasingly pursued my passion for two things—first, trying to understand the New Testament, and secondly, the blues. Despite having a career in the software industry, I completed my BD and PhD studies in universities in London and Belfast and have taught the New Testament for a number of years at my local university. I've a particular interest in the writings of the Apostle Paul. But my interest in the blues has increased in recent years as well, and I love listening to and playing the blues (I'm an enthusiastic, if not skilled guitar-ist) and reading blues history. But it never occurred to me until recently that it might be possible to combine in some ways these two passions and to be able to reflect on Christian theology through the lens of the blues.

A few years ago a new minister, Steve Stockman, came to our church in Belfast. I discovered he had written a couple of books on the connec-tions between secular rock music and Christian faith. Steve is passionate about music and, with his encouragement, the church has put on a number of musical evenings, where we have explored the music of various artists and have reflected on the ways in which their songs are relevant to faith—challenging, encouraging, or questioning. We are now running an annual blues evening, which has been a great success, with lots of great live blues music, along with critical reflection on matters of life and faith. The experi-ence of these evenings has encouraged me to begin to reflect on both blues music and my Christian faith more deeply and, in particular, on how we might think about various aspects of the Christian gospel. So this book is an attempt to think about the gospel through the lens of the blues—to see if there might be angles and ways of thinking about faith through a connection with the blues that might be both challenging and beneficial in considering the meaning of the gospel of Jesus Christ in today's world.

In his excellent *Getting the Blues*, which looks at what blues music might have to teach us about suffering and salvation, Stephen Nichols quotes third-century church father Tertullian, who said "What hath Athens to do with Jerusalem?," and reframes it as, "What has Christianity to do with the Mississippi Delta?" Nichols feels that Tertullian's negative answer to this question about the relationship between philosophy and faith was mistaken and that it would also be wrong to suggest that there should be no engagement between Christian faith and modern culture. Instead, there needs to be an engagement that is a "two-way street; we find common ground to speak the gospel to others and from others we gain a better understanding of the gospel."[1] That being the case, Nichols argues that Mississippi has rather a lot to do with Jerusalem.

Christianity and Cultural Engagement

For many years in a large section of the Christian church there has been deep suspicion of engaging in any meaningful way with modern culture. In the circles in which I grew up, much was made of "being *in* the world" but not being "*of* the world." What this meant in practice was that Christians should confine themselves to the sanctified world of the church and leave unredeemed culture well alone. So things like the cinema, rock concerts, certain types of literature, and popular music were all pretty much off-limits. Things have changed enormously, of course, but there is still an inward-looking Christian subculture where it seems safe for Christians to dwell, where faith is not challenged and where Christians can remain untainted by the "sinful" outside world. In this version of Christianity, the gospel is simply about a person understanding she or he is a sinner, repenting, exercising faith in Christ's death on her or his behalf, receiving forgiveness, being put right with God and bound for heaven after death.

The problem is, such an individualistic and other-worldly focus doesn't do justice to the full reality of the gospel, which has as much to do with world-transformation as it does to do with personal transformation. As we will see, the gospel we find in our New Testament, preached by both Jesus and Paul, is about the arrival of the rule of God on earth, about God renewing the cosmos and reconciling all things to Godself through Christ. It's about God putting things to rights—or, to put it another way, bringing justice. Once we start thinking about the gospel in this way, the focus shifts from the individual (although of course, importantly including the individual) and we see that there is not a part of our world that God does not wants to touch, redeem, and transform. And that God wants God's people to be a part of that redeeming, transformative project.

The story in the first few chapters of Genesis, for sure, tells us about a world gone wrong, about human beings who have given up their God-given

1. Nichols, *Getting the Blues*, 20.

task of representing God to God's world and taking responsibility for that world, because of their own desire for independence from God. The ramifications of that are far-reaching and include broken human relationships, broken societies, injustice at every turn, and broken responsibilities towards the earth. As Bob Dylan says simply, "Everything is broken."

God's plan for his world is nothing less than complete redemption for fallen human beings and a fallen cosmos. The Bible is the story of the creator's plan to deal with the problem of evil and to restore the order of God's world. As New Testament scholar Tom Wright maintains, God's plan was always to do this through a people. Despite the failure of God's ancient people to be God's agents of transformation, God's purpose was achieved through the one who represented Israel, Jesus, the Messiah—through his death and resurrection. Now this transformative project, which God will complete when Jesus returns, is to be moved forward by those who are, according to Paul, "in Christ."

Jesus followers are to be those who show what this new, changed world will be like—here and now. So Christian mission becomes more than simply appealing to individuals to respond in faith to Christ. It becomes an active engagement of God's people with culture, politics, society, and issues of justice, bringing the upside-down values of God's kingdom and Christ's love to bear wherever we can. The death and resurrection of Jesus, according to Paul, has resulted in "new creation," where all things have become new. It's a far-reaching idea that really does mean "all things," in terms of the scope of what God wants to make new.

Our engagement with the world is, however, as Nichols has pointed out, not a one-way process. Jesus talked about providing aid to the helpless and those in need and finding out that as much as we do it to them, we do it to him. Somehow as we engage with the poor and the disadvantaged, we find Jesus is their midst. And we ourselves are changed in the process. As we get involved in working to relieve suffering and combat injustice, it's not just those for whom we are working that are changed. In this very process of bringing compassion and justice, our own lives are transformed.

So too with the arts—Steve Stockman, in his book *The Rock Cries Out*, talks about finding "eternal truth in unlikely music." He maintains that there is much in the music of contemporary artists that is "saturated with spiritual context and redemptive messages that can teach life-changing truth to the believer and spiritual seeker alike."[2] Michael Gilmour in *Gods and Guitars*

2. Stockman, *The Rock Cries Out*, back cover copy.

approaches song lyrics as texts and finds it remarkable that, in music that has no connection to organized religion, there is to be found a great deal of meaningful spirituality and engagement with religious questions.[3]

In Christian Scharen's recent book, *Broken Hallelujahs*, he warns against looking at popular music as spiritually dangerous, and argues for a more positive engagement with something that is to be seen as part of God's good creation, albeit broken and damaged. He quotes Psalm 139:7–8 to suggest that we might routinely find evidence for God's presence in the midst of this broken creation:

> Is there any place I can go to avoid your Spirit?
> To be out of your sight?
> If I climb to the sky, you're there!
> If I go underground, you're there.

Scharen suggests the need to "surrender" to a work of art in order to engage imaginatively and properly with it. "If we attend to what sorts of people we are as a result of an encounter with [the artist], and how we describe the nature of our opinions in relation to what [the artist] has actually done," then we are able to encounter the art in a discerning, knowing way that goes far beyond simply reacting to it on the grounds of "taste." In this way, Scharen argues "we are enabled to give ourselves away to a broken and hurting world, seeking to understand it, love it, and ultimately share in its midst God's ongoing work of reconciliation." In the process, we ourselves are changed for the better.[4]

The gospel of Jesus Christ, then, is much wider in its scope and concerns than individuals' salvation. It's a message of hope for the whole world, a coming transformation, a transformation that God's people are called to participate in right now, engaging with all aspects of the life of this world, seeking to bring something of the life and love of God to bear on it and seeking to understand more of God through it.

The Blues and the Gospel

And so the blues, as with almost every other genre of music, is an appropriate area for Jesus followers to engage. Given the rich history of blues music and its genesis in black suffering, we might expect to find here a deep well

---

3. Gilmour, *Gods And Guitars*.

4. Scharen, *Broken Hallelujahs*, 130, 131, 137; from chapter 7, "Practicing Surrender."

from which to draw in reflecting on matters of faith. We might expect to find insights, challenges, and resonances with Christian faith. And that is just what we are going to find as we explore the blues in succeeding chapters. We're going to find that the blues is a very useful jumping-off point from which to reflect on the wide scope of the Christian gospel we've just begun to consider.

It is the case, of course, that whatever else we want to say about the blues, from its earliest days, whether it was the early women blues artists playing large shows or country blues artists playing juke joints, blues was entertainment. It was music to dance to, to drink to on a Saturday night, to help you forget the harshness of everyday life on the sharecropper's farm. That being the case, the blues and the church have often sat uneasily together. In the rural South, the church was an important part of life, a stabilizing influence on the community, and many churchgoers condemned the blues as sinful. It was the devil's music. It's not hard to understand why—with its myths of musicians going to the crossroads to sell their souls to the devil, the idea of "mojo" magic (originally a voodoo charm, but then coming to refer to sexual prowess), and associations with hard liquor drinking, blues music was difficult to reconcile with a churchgoing lifestyle. Michael Bane, in his book, *White Boy Singin' the Blues*, says,

> The blues especially were the opposite side of sacred. . . .
> You could sing gospel or the blues, but never both. The blues
> belonged to the Devil, with his high-rollin' ways . . . and if you
> sang his music, the door to the Lord's house was shut to you.[5]

The relationship between the church and the blues, however, was not quite so one-dimensional as Bane makes out. Blues artists went back and forth between careers as preachers and blues performers, and churches hosted blues artists—Blind Willie McTell from Georgia was one who often performed his music in a church setting. Plenty of blues musicians—Son House, Skip James, and Bill Broonzy, for example—were preachers before they were bluesmen. And some left the blues for the church—Georgia Tom, for example, recorded bawdy secular music before leaving behind the blues to record several hundred sacred songs and become the father of gospel music.

The blues, to be sure, was entertainment, but the blues has always expressed something deep about human life. It includes the whole gamut

5. Bane, *White Boy Singing the Blues*, 39.

of human experience—deep sorrow and lament, rage, resentment, murder, right through to joy, hope, and victory. The blues has always had the power to touch people deeply and they are music that seems to resonate at the deepest levels of our souls. This earthy, gritty nature of the blues is not something for Christians to shy away from—rather it is all the more reason to want to engage deeply with the blues, for in the blues we come face-to-face with real, human life-struggle, discrimination, imprisonment, violence, and poverty, with ramblin', no good, drunken men with unfaithful women—these are all the subject of the blues. All human life is here.

It seems to me, then, that the blues might very well be a very interesting and, indeed, appropriate place from which to consider the gospel of Jesus Christ, a gospel that itself has much to say about failed human beings, suffering, sorrow, justice, joy, and hope.

What Is the Blues?

So, to start off—what is the blues? If you're a musician, especially a guitarist, the blues means things like the pentatonic scale, flattened thirds, fifths, and sevenths, bent notes, and such like. But beyond the technical details, what is it really all about?

Robert Johnson, King of the Delta Blues, said "the blues is a low-down shakin' chill, it's a achin' old heart disease." Son House said the blues was something between a man and a woman. Memphis Willie widened it out, saying, "A blues is about something that's real. It's about what a man feels about some disappointment that happens that he can't do anything about." More profoundly, Furry Lewis of Memphis said, "All the blues, you can say, is true."[6] But perhaps the most important definition of the blues comes from B. B. King: "The blues is an expression of anger against shame and humiliation."[7]

He said that because, at heart, the essence of the blues is rooted in human suffering, in grief, in distress. The blues was rooted in the hardship, toil, injustice, and bondage of African Americans. Throw in bitterness, anger, broken relationships, sex, and virtually every aspect of life and you've basically got the blues.

6. Charters, *The Poetry of the Blues*, 12.

7. King, *Blues All Around Me*, 213.

B. B. King's "Why I Sing the Blues" (1969) locates the blues firmly in the context of slavery, injustice, and poverty. He starts off by reminding us of where it all started:

> When I first got the blues
> They brought me over on a ship
> Men were standing over me
> And a lot more with a whip.

The injustices suffered by the black community in the US, of course, didn't stop with the abolition of slavery. B. B. goes on to talk about the lack and poverty that was the lot for his community:

> I've laid in a ghetto flat
> Cold and numb
> I heard the rats tell the bedbugs
> To give the roaches some.

And in case there was any doubt as to the widespread nature of black suffering, King sings:

> I caught me a bus uptown, baby
> And every people, all the people
> Got the same trouble as mine.

The experience of poverty was compounded by the criminal justice system in the South, where simply being black increased an innocent man's chance of falling foul of the police:

> Blind man on the corner
> Begging for a dime
> The rollers come and caught him
> And throw him in the jail for a crime.

And that's why I sing the blues, says B. B. King:

> I got the blues
> Mm, I'm singing my blues
> I've been around a long time
> Mm, I've really paid some dues.

Where the blues started for many people was with a certain W. C. Handy, bandleader of a successful black orchestra, on a railway platform in Tutwiler, Mississippi, in 1903. As Handy waited for his train, he heard the sound of a man in tattered clothes playing a guitar in a most unusual fashion—he was sliding a pocketknife up and down the strings, creating a strange sound. For Handy the combination of the sliding guitar, the wailing voice, the repeated lyrics and the emotional intensity was incredibly powerful. "The effect," he said, "was unforgettable."[8] Handy first encountered the blues in the Mississippi Delta and it was on the Delta farms and in other Southern states like Arkansas, Louisiana, Texas, and the Carolinas that the blues took root in the first couple of decades of the twentieth century.

The Mississippi Delta was ideal as a breeding ground for the blues—it was here that a large black community lived and worked, struggling with poverty and the back-breaking work. The Delta soil, in a rich alluvial plane is, it is said, as thick as tar in some parts. While a few white people thrived on it, a whole lot of black people who worked on it were completely impoverished. Tommy Johnson, Charley Patton, Son House, Skip James, B. B. King, Howlin' Wolf, Muddy Waters, John Lee Hooker—musicians we associate with the birth of the blues—were just some of the artists who toiled on the land in the heat of the Mississippi sun. In the early decades of the twentieth century, African Americans worked on cotton and sugarcane farms, in what for most were pitiful conditions—long, back-breaking work for very little pay. Grandparents and parents of the first blues artists had been slaves; their children, though notionally free, were still living in conditions that were coercive and repressive.

James Cone, professor of theology at Union Seminary in New York, says the blues is the artistic response to the chaos of life. He says that no black person can escape the blues, because the blues is an inherent part of black existence in America. To be black, he says, is to be blue. As Leadbelly, ex-convict and country bluesman, said, "All negroes like the blues . . . because they was born with the blues."[9]

W. C. Handy said simply, "The blues were conceived in aching hearts."[10] Songs like Blind Lemon Jefferson's "Broke and Hungry," Leadbelly's "Pick a Bale of Cotton," Leroy Carr's "How Long Blues" ("I ain't seen no greenback on a dollar bill, How long, how long, baby how long?"), Victoria Spivey's "T.B. Blues" ("I got a tuberculosis; Consumption is killing me. It's too late, too late, too late, too late, too late")—and many, many more—all speak of the harshness of life for African Americans. All of this was the result of

8. Handy, *Father of the Blues*, 73–74.

9. Quoted in Shaw, *The World of the Soul*, 31.

10. Handy, *Father of the Blues*, 79.

poverty and discrimination, leading to ill-health, high infant mortality, family breakdown, and a whole host of social ills.

It's hardly surprising, really, that the blues emerged when and how it did. It was at once an expression of the sorrow and hardships of life for black communities in the South and a means of escape from those very trials.

The blues was part of life. It was sung at socials, parties, and juke joints—small, rural shacks where black people converged on Saturday nights to drink cheap whiskey and dance. As we have noted, although the blues may be thought of as an art form or as an expression of deep feeling, the early performers, be they successful, colorful stars like some of the women blues artists or more raw, rural blues singers, were entertainers who wanted their audiences to dance. How better, after six long days working hard to grow your own food and some cash crops for which you earned very little, to escape for a few hours on a Saturday night than with good company, music, and something to eat and drink.

So although we might say that the essence of the blues is rooted in human suffering, in grief, in distress, the blues is not simply a wallowing in all of that—it is just as much an expression of anger and hope that rails against the problems facing us, and that enables us to get to a place where we can rise above it all. And the blues deals with all of life. It's all there in what are lyrically quite simple songs—although in their own way, quite profound. And I guess that's one of the things that still draws us to the blues.

So—how does all this relate to Christian faith? What does the Delta have to do with Jerusalem? What does the crying and the hollering and the complaining and the raw expression of everyday life in the blues have to do with the gospel of Jesus Christ?

And the answer is—quite a lot, as we will discover as this book proceeds. There are two basic reasons. One is that, actually, the Bible has rather a lot of the blues in it. Stories of relationships, sex, murder, complaints to God, cries for deliverance, aspirations for a better future—it's all there, Genesis to Revelation. And the second reason is, as we have noted, the gospel is a big subject, encompassing all of human life and revolving around God's plan to transform God's world. The gritty, everyday expression of the blues, embedded deeply in the sorrows and joys of human experience, therefore, should give us good grounds for considering the transformative good news of Jesus Christ.

The Blues in the Bible

With respect to the blues in the Bible, we only need to look at the Psalms, for example—Israel's hymn book—to see a clear reflection of what we know as the blues. The Psalms actually might be better termed Israel's Blues Book. Here are some of the things the Psalmists write:

> For when I kept silent, my bones wasted away
> Through my groaning all day long (Ps 32:3).

> I am weary with my moaning
> Every night I flood my bed with tears (Ps 6:6).

> I am distraught by the noise of the enemy
> Because of the oppression of the wicked
> For they bring trouble against me (Ps 55:2–3).

> For I am ready to fall
> And my pain is ever with me (Ps 38:17).

> I was afflicted and about to die from my youth on
> The terrors have destroyed me (Ps 88:15–16).

> In vain I have kept my heart pure
> For I have been stricken all day long
> And chastened every morning (Ps 73:13–14).

A quick look at these verses from a range of Psalms is enough to convince us, I think, that the Psalmists have the blues. Any of these could fit neatly into almost any blues song you care to mention—and many of the blues verses could likewise be slotted into the Psalms—Bessie Smith's "I can't move no more; there ain't a place for an old girl to go to" ("Back Water Blues"); Blind Willie McTell's "Since my mother died and left me all alone, All my friends have forsaken me, People I haven't even got a home" ("Death Room Blues"); or Mississippi John Hurt's "I'm just an orphan, where my folks is I don't know, With my heavy burden, Lord, I wished I was dead" ("Blue Harvest Blues").

Many of the Psalms are written from the experience of Jewish people in exile. Their land was conquered, their holy city and temple destroyed, they were transported to live in a land of pagans who had no regard for their traditions—God seemed to have abandoned them. It's enough to make you sing the blues, isn't it? And that's exactly what they did—Psalm 137 records it for us—"By the rivers of Babylon, There we sat down and wept; We hung our guitars [Okay, it says "lyres" in the original] upon the willows." That's the blues all right. And don't forget the anger at the end of the Psalm—"O daughter Babylon, how blessed will be the one who repays you . . . who seizes and dashes your little ones against the rock."

And of course, there is that other Old Testament blues book—Job. Job was a man who was "blameless and upright" yet suffered terribly, and who protested against a theology that claimed that God punishes people in proportion to their disobedience and rewards them for their obedience.

The prophetic literature in the Bible, too, is shot through with the blues. Bemoaning the state of his people, Jeremiah cries:

> Raise a dirge;
> Eyes run down with tears
> Eyelids flow with water (Jer 9:18).

And actually, we could read many Old Testament passages where God's people get frustrated, get downcast, lament the state of affairs they find themselves in, suffer defeat after defeat, and cry out to God, sometimes in faith for deliverance, sometimes just in utter despair and complaint—and sometimes, as with the Psalmist, the cry for justice becomes a cry for revenge on the oppressors.

The prophets of Israel, in particular, knew that it was no use being in denial about the disastrous state of the world and of God's people. For them it was important to speak out the truth of the matter and thus to confront the oppressive powers of alienation, acquisitiveness, self-indulgence, and refusal to face reality that gripped priests, politicians, and people in their societies. Their speaking out—their truth-telling—about the reality of the world can be compared to the blues, which rises up from the experience of a world gone deeply wrong. Furry Lewis was right—the blues does indeed speak the truth.

When we turn to the New Testament, too, we find the blues: Jesus promised his followers persecution for seeking justice; he said people would revile them and slander them just for following him; he expected his followers to mourn for the state of the world and to deny themselves and take up a cross as he did. When we read Paul's letters to the first churches we find ourselves face-to-face with people who suffered poverty, adverse living conditions, and opposition from their neighbors. Paul describes himself as hungry and thirsty, poorly dressed, buffeted, and homeless (1 Cor 4:11). His list of adverse conditions in Romans 8—tribulation, distress, persecution, famine, nakedness, danger, the sword—are not hypothetical; they describe the real perils of the life of Paul and his fellow Jesus followers in the context of the Roman Empire.

The Blues, the Gospel, and Hope

Of course, as we'll see, telling the truth about the harsh realities of life is not where the Bible leaves things—there is an alternative narrative of hope and joy that is even now challenging the way things are and pointing the way to an alternative tomorrow.

We said earlier that the gospel is about God's plan to transform God's world and to deal with the problem of evil. The gospel both points to the fact that the world is broken and to the hope that God will transform the world. The Bible talks about this in terms of the reign of God coming to the earth. This was the hope of the Jewish prophets who longed for the "Day of the Lord," when Israel's God would decisively enter history and bring in the blessed day of his reign. The word the Old Testament uses to describe the blessings to be experienced in that day is the Hebrew word *shalom*, often translated "peace." The meaning of shalom goes far beyond the absence of strife, and is more about the flourishing of humanity and creation. The Day of the Lord, the day of shalom, was to be a day of well-being in body and mind, of abundance, of joy and satisfaction in all of life.

For the first Christians, this new day had broken into the present because of the life, death, and resurrection of Jesus the Messiah—meaning that the present reality of oppression, injustice, inhumanity, fear, and trouble was in the process of passing away. A new day was beginning to dawn, giving Jesus followers hope for a renewed creation, where peace, justice, joy, and glory would replace the struggles of this present age. As we will see, this is not just a hope for escape out of this world, but a hope for a transformed world and a call to anticipate and play our part in God's transformation project.

The blues, too, is not just about struggle, heartache, and truth-telling about injustice. The blues has always had a sense of hope, of anticipating a better day. Willie King, Mississippi bluesman, talking about the early Delta blues said, "the good Lord in his spirit had to send somethin' down to the people to help ease they worried mind. And that where the music come in—it would work in what you tryin' a do, what you strivin' for, to help give you a vision of a brighter day way up ahead, to help you get your mind offa what you are in right now . . . and the blues, like John Lee Hooker says, is a healer."[11] So the blues is partly about suffering and partly about hope.

That being the case, then, thinking about the blues—the history, the artists, the songs—might just be good stimulation for thinking about the Christian gospel. Both are about a world gone wrong, about injustice, about the human condition, and both are about hope for a better world.

Listening Guide

If you're new to the blues, a good place to start is with some modern exponents of the blues, who play both traditional blues and their own material. You might like to try the following:

Eric Bibb, *Spirit & the Blues*, Opus, 1994

B. B. King and Eric Clapton, *Riding with the King*, Reprise, 2000

Keb' Mo', *Martin Scorsese Presents*, Okeh, 2003

Guy Davis, *Red House*, Legacy, 2004

11. From interview with Martin Scorsese, director, *Feel Like Going Home.*

two

Suffering, the Gospel, and the Blues

Blessed are those who mourn,
for they will be comforted.

Matthew 5:4

The Context of the Blues

The blues was born in the Southern states of the US in the context of the legalized discrimination and injustice that followed slavery, the Civil War, and Reconstruction. James Cone suggests that "the blues is the experience of being black in a white racist society."[1]

By 1877, white Southern Democrats had regained political power in every Southern state and they began to enact laws that segregated black people from white. These so-called "Jim Crow" laws (Jim Crow was a pejorative expression for blacks) at state and local levels remained in force until 1965. African Americans were segregated from whites in all public facilities across the South and said to be "separate but equal."[2] In reality, this simply disadvantaged black people in every conceivable way—economically, educationally, and socially—and was backed up by legislation and the police.

So blacks were not allowed to use the same schools, public places, public transport, restrooms, restaurants, or drinking fountains as whites. In addition, blacks became effectively disenfranchised, as a result of restrictive

1. Cone, *The Spirituals and the Blues*, 103.
2. *Plessy v. Ferguson*, United States Supreme Court, 1896.

voter registration and electoral rules. The growth of the beginnings of a thriving black middle class was stunted. Bigotry and anti-black sentiment was rife, with blacks being blamed for the failure of the South in the Civil War.

In short, African Americans were relegated to the status of second-class citizens. They were routinely referred to in newspapers and magazines as niggers, coons, and darkies. Blacks were oppressed, marginalized, and made to suffer indignity, poverty, and hopelessness, and were kept down at the bottom by the threat of violence, either by the authorities themselvs or legitimated by them.

Lynching became a means of terrorism of whites towards blacks, used to defend white domination and to intimidate and control blacks. It was usually done by hanging, but also by burning at the stake. By conservative estimates, 3,500 African Americans were lynched in the United States between 1882 and 1968, mostly from 1882 to 1920. Those responsible for the lynching were seldom arrested and many police were complicit in what went on.[3] At times there were mass lynchings, effectively pogroms, where white mobs stormed through black communities, killing and destroying property. In 1919, "race riots" such as these occurred in 26 American cities, with eleven people being burned alive and many more killed by other means.

For many whites, lynching was defensible and necessary. South Carolina governor and later US senator Cole Blease said that lynching was the "divine right of the Caucasian race to dispose of the offending blackamoor without the benefit of jury."[4]

Billie Holiday famously recorded a song about lynching, entitled "Strange Fruit" in 1939. The song is almost too graphic to bear:

> Southern trees bear a strange fruit,
> Blood on the leaves and blood at the root,
> Black body swinging in the Southern breeze,
> Strange fruit hanging from the poplar trees.

It goes on to talk about "The bulging eyes and the twisted mouth," and, "the sudden smell of burning flesh."

This is the original protest song. It is simple, sparse but effective. It depicts lynching in all of its brutality. The song articulated the growing

3. Raper, *The Tragedy of Lynching.*

4. Cited in Gussow, *Seems Like Murder Here,* 49.

awareness and anger at what went on in the Southern states that was to find expression in the rise of the mass civil rights movement of the 1950s and 1960s. *phân biệt chủng tộc ở da màu*

Lynching was widespread and common in the South during the Jim Crow period and blacks lived in terror for their lives because of its capricious nature. Looking at a white woman the "wrong way" or acting in a way that was perceived "uppity" was sometimes all it took to begin inciting whites to form a lynch mob. Bluesman Skip James said simply, "They'd lynch you in a minute."[5] Simply being out and about in the evening in the many "sundown towns" in the South could be fatal for blacks who ignored the signs warning, "Nigger, don't let the sun set on your head."[6]

Self-defense or protest were not options, so resistance was broadly confined to the blues and religion. "At the juke joints on Friday and Saturday nights and at churches on Sunday mornings and evening week nights blacks affirmed their humanity and fought back against dehumanization."[7]

The constant threat of being lynched is arguably referred to in "Hellhound on my Trail," recorded by Robert Johnson in 1937:

> I got to keep movin', I got to keep movin'
> Blues fallin' down like hail
> And the day keeps on worryin' me,
> There's a hellhound on my trail.

The ever-present threat of lynching also crops up in a number of blues songs about hangmen. Blind Lemon Jefferson's "Hangman's Blues" from 1928 is an example:

> Mean ole hangman is waitin' to tighten up the noose
> Lord I'm so scared I'm tremblin' in my shoes.

Adam Gussow makes the point that fear of white reprisal "inhibited early blues singers from addressing lynching directly" but that the terror of lynching was encoded in a great many classic and country blues songs.[8]

When the blues began to develop around 1900 or so, slavery was just a generation away and for many blacks working on the farms in Mississippi, their lot had hardly improved. They worked as sharecroppers on tobacco and cotton farms, in a desperately unfair system doing back-breaking work

5. Ibid., 53.

6. Cone, *The Cross and the Lynching Tree*, 12.

7. Ibid.

8. Gussow, *Seems like Murder Here*, 11.

from dawn to dusk, with little return for their efforts. Many were effectively enslaved in timber camps, mines, and farms in what was known as "peonage," a new form of slavery. In the days of antebellum slavery, music had been of enormous importance to the black community—James Cone refers to it as "the power of song in the struggle for black survival."[9] He goes on to say that black music "unites the joy and the sorrow, the love and the hate, the hope and the despair of black people."[10] The slave spirituals were often long and mournfully slow chants, reflecting the sadness and despair of people who were oppressed and in dire straits. W. E. B. Du Bois calls them "sorrow songs."[11]

> Oh Lord! Oh My Lord!
> Oh My Good Lord! Keep me from sinkin' down . . .
> Nobody knows the trouble I've seen . . .
> I'm bowed down with a burden of woe
> O who will deliver po' me?

According to one slave who escaped, Frederick Douglass, the slave songs were "of a plaintive cast, and told a tale of grief and sorrow. In the most boisterous outburst of rapturous sentiment, there was ever a tinge of deep melancholy."[12]

This sense of sorrow and mourning because of injustice is a major theme in the Old Testament. One example is found in the book of the prophet-poet Micah, who in the eighth century BC was concerned about aggressive real estate acquisitiveness by the wealthy who cared little for those they dispossessed:

> Alas for those who devise wickedness and evil deeds on their beds! . . .
> They covet fields, and seize them;
> Houses and take them away;
> They oppress householder and house,
> People and their inheritance (Mic 2:1–2).

His contemporary prophet, Hosea, blankly concludes of this state of affairs that "the land mourns" (Hos 4:3). Old Testament scholar Walter Brueggemann, commenting on this, says that "the land is reduced to

---

9. Cone, *The Spirituals and the Blues*, 1.

10. Ibid., 5.

11. Du Bois, *The Souls of Black Folk*, 182.

12. Douglass, "My Bondage and My Freedom," 83.

weeping sadness . . . it bespeaks a society out of control, alienated from God, set against the neighbour, passionate for its own advantage."[13]

The Psalms, of course, are full of such mourning, just as much as in any of the early blues songs:

> You have put me in the depths of the Pit
> In the regions dark and deep . . .
> You have caused friend and neighbor to shun me;
> My companions are in darkness. (Ps 88:6, 18)

> My heart is in anguish within me,
> The terrors of death have fallen upon me.
> Fear and trembling come upon me,
> And horror overwhelms me. (Ps 55:4–5)

A full one-third of the Psalms are laments. They give voice to cries from below of pain, anger, and need. They are visceral cries to God, expressing the deep sorrow and mourning of individuals and people in need. As such they resonate richly with the mourning and sorrow we find in the early blues, which, after slavery but still in the situation of oppression under the Jim Crow laws and all that went with them, enabled African Americans to make music to express their deep feelings and stories.

So, out of this musical heritage emerged the blues, what James Cone calls "a secular spiritual." Though not couched in the language of the Bible, blues songs are laments, in the same way as the spirituals. Spirituals such as "Nobody Knows the Trouble I've Seen" or "Sometimes I Feel Like a Motherless Child" were the forerunners to what were later called the "worried blues." Bluesman Huddie Ledbetter, better known as Leadbelly, noticed this trajectory, when he said, "Blues was composed up by the Negro people when they was under slavery. They was worried."[14]

The song "Worried Blues," attributed to Hally Wood, but possibly going back to Leadbelly, was also recorded by Bob Dylan (one of the most important blues artists of the twentieth century, though often not recognized as such) in 1962 and released in 1991 on *The Bootleg Series 1–3* (1991).[15] The song is sparse and its very simplicity strikes a note of despair:

> I got those worried blues, Lord
> I'm going where I never been before.

13. Brueggemann, *Disruptive Grace*, 165.

14. Ames, *The Story of American Folk Song*, 262.

15. Bob Dylan, *The Bootleg Series 1–3* (Columbia, 1991).

> ... I'm going where the chilly winds don't blow
> ... Listen to that cold whistle blow
> I'm going where I never been before.

Blind Lemon Jefferson, from Texas, one of the most popular blues artists of the 1920s, also has a "worried blues":

> Worried so bad, can't tell my stockin' from my shoes
> Worried so bad, can't tell my stockin' from my shoes
> I laid down last night with Lemon's lowdown worried blues.

His "Broke and Hungry Blues" also expresses the lament of the poor and downtrodden:

> I'm broke and hungry, ragged and dirty too
> I said I'm broke and hungry, ragged and dirty too
> I'm motherless, fatherless, sister and brotherless too.
> (Lemon's Worried Blues)

Blind Willie Johnson, blinded as a child, and who died a pauper in 1945 after living in the ruins of his burnt-down house, expresses a deep-rooted sorrow in "Lord I Just Can't Keep from Crying":

> When my heart's full of sorrow and my eyes are filled with tears
> Lord, I just can't keep from crying sometimes.

The blues were, and remain, a remarkable expression of human grief and mourning for whatever afflicts us. Often the problem is in sexual relationships—that was the essence of the blues, according to Son House—but it is impossible to limit the blues to this or to deny that the blues grew directly out of the experience of black suffering. As James Cone says, "The blues are about black life and the sheer earth and gut capacity to survive in an extreme situation of oppression."[16] In addition, Adam Gussow makes a good case for seeing the suffering, indignity, and injustice suffered by black Americans as *the* basis of the blues, and that the blues songs "unconsciously transcoded . . . inflicted traumas . . . fear, grief and anger." A song like *Hesitation Blues*—"Tell me how long will I have to wait, Can I get you now or will I hesitate"—according to Gussow is a "blues lament," which contains the idea of "speaking back to white violence."[17]

We have mentioned that mourning songs, laments if you will, are not just the territory of the blues, but are an important element in the record of

16. Cone, *The Spirituals and the Blues*, 97.
17. Gussow, *Seems Like Murder Here*, 59–65.

the life of God's people in the Old Testament. But what about the gospel—is there anything to do with mourning in it? First of all, we need to think about what the gospel actually is.

What Is the Gospel?

Walter Trout, one of the world's finest living exponents of electric blues, in his song "Brother's Keeper" on his 2012 album *Blues for the Modern Daze*, sings, "Jesus said to feed the hungry, Jesus said to feed the poor; So many of those so-called Christians, They don't believe in that no more." In the CD liner notes for this song, Trout talks about the callousness towards the poorer members of society of some of the politicians in the US, and how he has observed that attitude being applauded by "people who yell about how they're deep Christians." His view of that is that "they're losing sight of what their religion is supposed to be."

Trout, of course, is right—Jesus did indeed talk a great deal about feeding the hungry, extending hospitality to foreigners, and looking after the poor and those in prison. In fact, he made doing such things the criteria by which God judges. How come, then, we've gotten to the point where Walter Trout's observation about Christians rings true?

A large part of the answer to this is the sort of theology that has developed in modern Western societies. An influential American pastor and author, John Piper, recently asked the question, "Did Jesus preach the gospel?" He went on to answer this question, which might seem rather surprising to people outside the church, by trying to relate some of Jesus's teaching in the Gospels to the Apostle Paul's talk about justification by faith—the idea that people are put right with God only by virtue of their faith in Christ. Scot McKnight, commenting on this, finds a major problem with it—"Piper's assumption . . . that justification is the gospel."[18] Daniel Kirk suggests that if indeed the idea of personal salvation is the sum total of the Christian gospel, then we are left with "a rather perplexing collection of Christian artefacts known as 'the Gospels' which do not actually contain much of the gospel at all."[19]

We might well want to suggest that there is not the gulf between Jesus and his first interpreter, Paul the apostle, that recent popular literature has made out—the sort of thing that says, "Paul took the simple message of

18. McKnight, *The King Jesus Gospel*, 25.

19. Kirk, *Jesus Have I Loved, but Paul?*, 50.

Jesus, made it much more complicated and turned it into Christianity."[20] But Piper's attempt to shoehorn Jesus into Paul's idea of justification by faith misunderstands both Jesus and the apostle. There is more to the four Gospels in our New Testaments than just background material to the real story of Jesus's death, resurrection, and ascension back to heaven. For many Christians the Gospel stories are valuable only because they portray a wonder-working Jesus, important because this is indicative of Jesus's deity.[21] Beyond that, and perhaps some general, timeless principles we might glean from Jesus's teaching, the Gospels are seen as somewhat peripheral to the clear gospel that Paul preached of personal sin, inability to help ourselves, salvation from sin and guilt, and a home awaiting us in heaven in the skies.

So when we read an account of Jesus's Sermon on the Mount in Matthew's Gospel (chapters 5–7), we might be excused for wondering what on earth is going on. Jesus nowhere talks about personal sin or guilt and doesn't mention anything about the saving value of his death (and bear in mind, Jesus gets pretty explicit to his followers that at some stage he *is* going to run into trouble and be executed). Through the history of the church, Christians have gone through all sorts of hoops trying to explain (explain away?) the Sermon on the Mount. Sixteenth-century reformer Martin Luther took the view that Jesus's demands here are clearly impossible for us and so their aim is to drive us to despair at our own efforts at goodness and into Christ's arms. More recently, the church I grew up in figured there was such a disjunction between Jesus's teaching here and the rest of the New Testament that it must be irrelevant until the arrival of some future millennial kingdom. And then there was a more scholarly view put forward in the early part of the twentieth century by French physician, philosopher, and theologian Albert Schweitzer, who suggested Jesus's teaching in the Sermon was given by Jesus to his followers in a mistaken expectation by him that the end of the world was coming imminently. So the Sermon and Jesus's teachings generally were not intended to be used by later generations. Something broadly similar has been advanced more recently by other scholars.[22]

All of this, however, seems deeply unsatisfactory, so how should we read Jesus's Sermon in Matthew's Gospel? We need to read the Sermon,

20. A typical example of this sort of approach is Wilson, *The Mind of Paul the Apostle*.

21. Wright, *When God Became King*, 53ff.

22. E.g., Crossan, *The Historical Jesus*, which suggests that the Sermon on the Mount was a blueprint for life in a Galilean village without reference to any larger program or agenda.

first of all, against its historical context in Jesus's life. Is there a way to read the Sermon, and indeed Jesus's life, that is faithful to Jesus's world of first-century Palestine and is integrated with the overall narrative of scripture?

Jesus's life and teaching really only make proper sense when seen against the Jewish tradition and background of which he was a part. So when he arrives in Galilee proclaiming the arrival of the kingdom or rule of God (Mark 1:17), he is tapping in to a rich seam of Jewish thought and expectation.[23]

There was a ready expectation by many Jews in the first century that their God, Yahweh, would act once more in history to deliver them from their enemies. Their land may have been ruled by Roman pagans and many of their people scattered throughout the Roman Empire, but Jews held on to their belief, arising from their scriptures, that God, the creator God, the one true God, had graciously chosen them to be God's own people and had shown himself to be utterly faithful throughout their history, despite their own waywardness and faithlessness. That being the case, God would surely demonstrate his faithfulness again and decisively enter history on their behalf, as God had done at crucial points in their history—at the time of the exodus, when God rescued them from slavery in Egypt, and, more recently, when God had acted through the Maccabean rebellion in 166 BC to rid their sacred land of occupying pagans. God's action in history on God's people's behalf—God's faithfulness—is recounted again and again in the Old Testament (famously in the Psalms, e.g., Psalm 25:10: "All the paths of the Lord are steadfast love and faithfulness"). It was the basis of the hope that was expressed by Israel's prophets that God would act finally and decisively to bring in a new day of peace and blessing for God's people, and indeed, the world.

If we begin to understand Jesus against this background, then his teaching and actions begin to make sense. Jesus shared with his contemporaries the hope of the arrival of God's new age. What made him different from the various other groups who had their own ideas of how exactly all this might come about was that Jesus clearly thought that God's rule was arriving in and through his own person.[24]

---

23. Very helpful in this regard has been the recent output by N. T. Wright, noted first-century historian, New Testament scholar, and previously Bishop of Durham. See, e.g., Wright, *The New Testament and the People of God*, and *Jesus and the Victory of God*.

24. A good summary of the outlook and hopes of various Jewish sects of the period can be found in Wright, *The New Testament and the People of God*, chapter 10, "The Hope of Israel."

Matthew puts the big block of Jesus's teaching, which we call the Sermon on the Mount, right after the beginning of Jesus's activity in Galilee, where his gospel message was that the people should change their ways, because God's rule on earth was arriving.[25] Matthew then, clearly seeking to show how this indeed was the case, records Jesus performing miraculous healings and exorcisms. As far as our Gospel writers are concerned, Jesus's gospel—good news message—was about the arrival of the new age of God's peaceful rule on earth and that he himself was the means by which it was arriving. And Jesus's assault on the various ills of humanity that were experienced by the people in Galilee was the demonstration that this, indeed, was the case.

So then we come to the Sermon, starting at the beginning of chapter 5 of Matthew's gospel, which is clearly designed to show what Jesus's teaching about the "kingdom"—God's newly arriving rule—consisted of. This is Matthew's way of recording what Jesus said about how people should live, in the light of the now-arriving kingdom. What does changing your ways—repenting—because of the new reality in the world actually mean?

We are far away here from the idea that Jesus's teaching here is an impossible ethic designed to show how hopeless we are—what Jesus says in this "sermon" is designed to show us what the arriving rule of God looks like and how people who want to be part of that should live. So we get Jesus talking about a whole range of things—suffering, persecution, justice, peace, anger, sexuality, love of your enemies, prayer, anxiety, the faithfulness and love of God, and hypocrisy—topics with both personal impact and implications for wider society, but all demonstrating the way in which God's kingdom and those who choose to be a part of it look very different from the way things normally work in the world. As Donald Kraybill famously said—it's an upside-down kingdom.[26]

So the Sermon is an explanation of vital aspects of the gospel—the good news that God is bringing, through Jesus, his reign of peace and justice to the world.

25. From that time Jesus began to proclaim, "Repent, for the kingdom of heaven has come near" (Matt 4:17).

26. Kraybill, *The Upside Down Kingdom.*

"Blessed are those who mourn"

In verse 3–11 of Matthew chapter 5, we have what are commonly known as the "Beatitudes," which consist of a number of statements by Jesus which begin "blessed—or happy—are they . . ." Verse four says, "Blessed are those who mourn, for they shall be comforted."

Christians don't often talk about mourning—especially rich, Western Christians. We want to talk more about success, material blessing, rejoicing, staying upbeat—but mourning? What's that about? The gospel we've swallowed is an entirely personalized one where it's all about me, my relationship with God, my progress, my blessing.

Wealth and technology have put us in a position never before known by people in history. We all have some degree of control over our circumstances and we can make choices—all sorts of choices: where to live, what to study, who to marry, what career to follow, what sort of entertainment we'd like to consume, what to eat, how to spend our money . . . the list is endless. The wealthier we are, the more choices we have. And often our Christianity is simply a means of giving all this a holy gloss. Apart from making sure the choices we make don't involve certain types of sexual behavior, profanity, or addiction to drugs and alcohol, all we really want is to know what God's will is for the choices we make in life. We may not go as far as the "prosperity gospel" proponents in suggesting that God wants to multiply our choices and possible beneficial outcomes, but, sure as anything, we really don't want our Christian faith to upset the applecart of "our way of life."[27]

The thing is, though, the majority of the world's Christians do not live in places where they have the choices and possibilities that we do. When you live in poverty, your choices become very limited, down to the very necessities of life, sometimes simply to eating and drinking clean water. Lack of choice caused by poverty makes poor people more easily exploited, which in turns maintains poverty—it's a vicious circle.

Today, a full 50 percent—yes, *50 percent*—of the world lives on less than $2 a day. According to the World Health Organization, currently one-third of the world is underfed, and one-third is starving. Every year, 35 percent of children's deaths in the world are caused by malnutrition. Just because it doesn't reach our TV news or we're too busy to notice it doesn't

27. "Our way of life" was what President George Bush said was the thing threatened in the wake of the terrorist attacks of 9/11. In early 2012, Nicholas Sarkozy, ex-president of France, said that the presidential election was all about "preserving our way of life."

alter the fact—we live on a small island of prosperity floating on a great sea of poverty and need.

The truth is that mourning may not be very much part of our lives, but it is part of daily life for billions of people on the planet. From time to time, mourning breaks into our lives abruptly, when a loved one dies. And to be sure there are all sorts of griefs and heartaches that we face as we go through life. We don't, however, think that it's the norm, or should be the norm. For people living in poverty, though, where children die because of malnourishment, malaria, diarrhea, or other preventable diseases, and where everyday existence is a major hurdle because of lack of shelter, medicine, clothing, and food, mourning is a way of life.

So what is it that Jesus is getting at here when he says that it's those who mourn who are blessed? What is it about the now-arriving rule of God that brings blessing to those who mourn?

The Need for Mourning Songs

We much prefer to think about success, achievement, improvement. Economic growth is the driver of the modern nation and national progress is measured in gross domestic product (GDP) growth. When we read our newspapers and watch our TVs, we are bombarded with stories that highlight the success or otherwise of the economy and with advertisements selling us stuff that (so it is claimed) will improve our lifestyles and make us happier. Everything, it seems, puts the focus on us—our happiness, our success, our betterment. This is just the dynamic of the modern democratic, capitalist nation state—that's the way it works, and it's hard to quiet the noise it makes or to resist it forcing us into its mold. There is little to force us to hear the lament of the poor, the desperate—the great mass people in the world who, like the African Americans during the days when the blues began to emerge, cry out for relief and justice. It's not easy to be attentive to that cry for clean water, for enough food for the day, relief from the catastrophe of global warming, or from the tyranny of war.

But, as Stephen Nichols says, "the blues and the Bible . . . force us to listen more deeply and honestly."[28] As we have seen, the Bible has a considerable amount of mourning and lamenting in it, of those in distress and despair crying out to God for salvation and deliverance.

---

28. Nichols, *Getting the Blues*, 41.

Kathleen O'Connor, Old Testament scholar, in a book about the Old Testament Book of Lamentations, comments upon our consumerist way of life that is deaf to the cry of the world:

> I am convinced that our profound spiritual hunger undermines not only our own humanity; it also affects our relationships with other peoples and with the earth itself. We feed that hunger in our frenzied self-centredness and with anesthetizing abundance and violence. This is the "spiritual catastrophe in which the rich live," and it continues to endanger the world. I find in Lamentations food for this hunger and a healing balm for hidden wounds. The hunger of the rich is not comparable to the material hungers of the poor, but our own humanity, or inability to be empathetic, and our denial of our own deep hungers directly impinge upon the lives of the poor who often have much to teach us about humanity.[29]

The ideology of our modern world numbs us—blues artist Walter Trout calls it the "modern daze:"

> You get yours
> I'll get mine
> Just make sure
> That you toe the line. ("Blues for the Modern Daze")

We desperately need to recover what it is to mourn, to lament. To do so "is an embrace of creaturely reality amid bewitching ideologies that benumb us."[30] Our culture is deeply resistant to lament, but to learn about lament is to learn about our own deep dependence upon God and to discover our deep relationship to brothers and sisters throughout the world who live in constant distress. We need to learn how to mourn.

The Blessing of Mourning

Water Brueggemann says that "the practice of lament is a sine qua non for believing people who embrace need and vulnerability in the presence of God." Lament, he says, needs to be "a permanent theological practice."[31]

The problem is that our individualistic, technology-driven world fools us into a false sense of self-reliance. We are prey to the continual bombardment of the message of economic growth from advertising and the news.

29. O'Connor, *Lamentations and the Tears of the World*, xiv.

30. Brueggemann, *Disruptive Grace*, 185.

31. Ibid.

We need to recover a sense of creaturely dependence upon the creator, and to hear again the decisive answer given by Jesus to the temptation to be self-reliant—"Human beings shall not live by bread alone, but by every word that comes from God" (Matthew 4:4).

A prime way of doing this is to connect in some meaningful way with the poor in the world. It's only as we turn our ears towards the loud lament that is coming from many quarters all over the world that we ourselves can begin to be free from the ensnaring tentacles of our consumerist culture.

Far too often Christians seem to be wrapped up in their own pious little world of interior spirituality. At times, even our activities around church life and events fool us into thinking we are being faithful Jesus followers. Jesus's words in Matthew 25 should thoroughly disabuse us of this idea—the criterion for God the judge at the great assize will be the attention we have paid to the cry of the hungry and the thirsty, the destitute, the sick, and the imprisoned.

Once we make this vital connection between our faith and the lament of the poor, we become free to see ourselves and our own world as they should be seen. We begin to realize that we, too, are those in need and who are equally dependent upon God. As we begin to walk alongside the poor in whatever way we can, we begin to see that, in the end, we are all God's creatures, dependent upon him for our very lives. We need to begin, then, not only to hear the lament of the poor, but to take up that lament with them and raise our united voices for justice and for change.

Kathleen O'Connor says of Israel's ancient Book of Lamentations,

> Lamentations is ancient poetry of truth-telling, an act of survival
> that testifies to the human requirement to speak the unspeakable
> . . . to assert boldly the "sheer fact of pain."[32]

The scriptures—especially the Psalms and the Prophets—are full of what we might call "truth-telling." This is a courageous, bold lament about the way the world is, no matter what may be the consequences from vested interests that do not want the truth to be told. We will explore this in more detail in the next chapter.

Blessed are those who mourn, then, says Jesus. For those who want to know the blessing of being a part of this newly arriving reign of God, mourning is a necessary component of life. How much have we allowed mourning to be part of our individual lives and the lives of our church

---

32. O'Connor, *Lamentations and the Tears of the World*, xiv.

communities? Are we so connected to the cry of the world that we hear that constant lament, in such a way that our lives and communal life are continually aligned with the God of the poor, the one who is the defender of the cause of the poor, the deliverer of the needy and the crusher of the oppressor (Ps 72:4)? To do this requires a conscious decision to live in a different way than seems natural and normal to us, given our culture—this is precisely what the Apostle Paul is getting at when he advises the Roman Christians to whom he was writing not to allow themselves to be molded into the pattern of the world around them, but rather to be transformed by thinking in a completely different way.

The blues was born amongst precisely the sort of poor, needy, and oppressed people that the Psalms talk about. As James Cone says,

> Because the black person had to live in the midst of a broken
> existence, the reality of the blues was stark and real.[33]

That's why it is such a powerful medium and has so much to teach us about the power of lament. The blues tells the uncomfortable truth about the world from the perspective of those below, and as such is an important genre for Christians to pay attention to—we need all the help we can get in learning once more about what it is to mourn about the state of the world. Because it's only as we do that we begin to understand how to be truly blessed in God's kingdom.

Listening Guide

Billie Holiday, *Strange Fruit and Greatest Hits (Remastered),* The Restoration Project, 2012

Robert Johnson, *King of the Delta Blues,* Sony, 1997

Leadbelly, *Midnight Special,* Prism, 2003

Walter Trout, *Blues for the Modern Daze,* Provogue, 2012

---

33. Cone, *The Spirituals and the Blues,* 109.

three

The Blues, Jesus, and Justice

Blessed are those who hunger and thirst after justice,
for they shall be satisfied.

MATTHEW 5:6

Injustice for Black Southerners

In those days, it was "Kill a mule, buy another; kill a nigger, hire another.
They had to have a license to kill anything but a nigger. We was always in
season." The was the sobering recollection of a black southerner's reflection
of life in the Mississippi Delta region in the 1930s.[1]

As we have seen already, the blues is rooted in the suffering of American blacks coming out of slavery into the long era of Jim Crow discrimination and ill treatment. So the blues is a window into one experience of
injustice in the world and reminds us of all the other experiences of hardship and suffering endured by many, many other groups in the world.

Slavery existed as a legal institution in North America for more than
a century before the founding of the United States in 1776, and continued
mostly in the South until the passage of the Thirteenth Amendment to the
United States Constitution in 1865. By 1860 the slave population in the
United States had grown to four million and it took a Civil War, in which
around 700,000 people died, to bring it to an end (although, as we shall see

---

1. Cited in Scheper-Hughes and Bourgois, *Violence in War and Peace*, 125.

in due course, slavery in another guise existed until 1945 in the Southern states).

Slavery was a wretched existence, where slaves were typically denied the opportunity to learn to read or write, were denied medical care, and were brutally punished by whipping, shackling, hanging, beating, burning, mutilation, branding, and imprisonment. Punishment and abuse was often meted out simply to assert the dominance of the master or overseer over the slave, and rape and sexual abuse were commonplace. Slavery effectively denied the humanity of the slave—a slave was not a person; she was a piece of property that you could do what you liked with.

The abolition of slavery, however, did not bring to an end black suffering. When emancipation became a legal reality, white Southerners were concerned with both controlling the newly freed slaves and keeping them in the labor force at the lowest level. They implemented something called convict leasing, which was just slavery under another name—African Americans had laws selectively applied to them and suffered from discriminatory sentencing, and often, as wrongly convicted prisoners, were forced to work without pay and with extraordinary physical coercion.

The question for African Americans, particularly in the Southern states, became, what does freedom really mean? Freed people continued to work under their former owners for nominal wages that made little real difference in their material well-being. For some, including freedwomen and their children, the elderly, and the sick, life actually became more hazardous, as they were thrown out of their homes by landowners reacting bitterly to the new "free labor" arrangements. The result was either scratching out a bare subsistence or dying in hunger and squalor. The whole system was coercive and repressive.

Institutionalized racial discrimination continued, as we saw in the last chapter, to afflict black people who suffered until the 1960s civil rights movement. Every black child in the Southern states in this period "would come to appreciate the terrible unfairness and narrowness of that world—the limited options, the need to curb ambition, to contain feelings, and to weigh carefully every word, gesture, and movement when in the presence of whites."[2]

The injustice took many forms and was built into the fabric of life. It might simply be a matter of being segregated on buses or railroad coaches. The young James Robinson, born in 1907, attempted to get on a bus in

2. Litwack, *Trouble in Mind*, 7.

Knoxville, Tennessee, and was roughly pulled back by a white person who shouted at him, "You damn little darkey, didn't anybody learn you to stay in your place? You get the hell back there and wait till the white people get on the bus. Give a nigger an inch and he'll take a mile."[3]

Blacks suffered violence or the threat of violence at the hands of whites. Richard Wright recalls how at age ten he began to feel a "dread of white people." "Nothing challenged the totality of my personality so much as this pressure of hate and threat that stemmed from the invisible whites. I would stand for hours on the doorsteps of neighbors' houses listening to their talk, learning how a white woman had slapped a black woman, how a white man had killed a black man. It filled me with awe, wonder, and fear."[4]

Blacks needed to be "kept in their place" and whites acted with impunity to ensure this was the case. Benjamin Mays remembered that as a boy in 1898, a crowd of armed whites came up to his father, drawing their guns and requiring him to remove his hat and bow down. Whites hated blacks being "sassy," "uppity," or "impudent."[5] This was the crime of a black man whom Martin Luther King Sr. saw beaten to death. The man's refusal to hand over his paycheck to a group of whites was perceived as "sassiness."[6] The threat of unprovoked violence was ever present. John Henry Corniggin was shot to death in 1917. His crime? Walking across a white man's melon patch.[7] The crime was never investigated.

Educational opportunities were denied to blacks, especially in the rural South. Schools there were very primitive, unpainted one-room buildings, and pupils sat on the floor or on benches made of split logs. Basic school supplies were denied. But in any case, often black children were required to work in the cotton fields rather than attend school for part of the year. Benjamin May, by age nineteen, could not recall having been in school more than four months in any year.[8] The obstacles to many black children gaining any sort of decent education were often formidable.

Work conditions were brutal. W. E. B. Du Bois recalls a conversation with a black farmer around the turn of the twentieth century, who told him, "The land was a little Hell. I've seen niggers drop dead in the furrow, but

3. Robinson, *Road Without Turning*, 41–43.
4. Wright, "Black Boy (American Hunger)," 180.
5. Mays, *Born to Rebel*, 1.
6. King Sr. with Riley, *Daddy King*, 29–31.
7. Murray, *Proud Shoes*, 262–65.
8. Mays, *Born to Rebel*, 7, 38.

they were kicked aside, and the plough never stopped."[9] Blacks worked the cotton fields in what Du Bois called "a mockery of freedom," in what was "forced labor practically without wages."[10] On prison farms, blacks were set to work, having been convicted of trivial crimes, simply to provide the labor needed by the state. The black man was seen "as the workhorse or mule of the South," and the objective was to get the most out of him at the least expense.[11] Black women in domestic service were worked brutally hard, getting up at dawn to prepare breakfast for the white family, preparing lunch and dinner and doing all the domestic chores in between times, on duty from sunrise to sundown. Whites wielded tremendous power over black labor and discipline was usually quick and ruthless, using, whenever necessary, the power of the police and the courts to keep the established order. Although there were blacks who managed to succeed in terms of wealth and property, for the most part everything was stacked against black people gaining the education and training needed to do anything but the most menial work.

Between 1890 and 1908, every state in the Deep South adopted a new state constitution explicitly for the purpose of disenfranchising blacks, a situation that was really only properly rectified in the 1960s. During this period, black people in the Southern states were systematically discriminated against on the basis of their color. Racial segregation resulted in excluding blacks from white company in street and railway cars, public toilets and water fountains, parks, theatres, and boarding houses. Blacks were virtually excluded from swimming pools, tennis courts, and bowling alleys. Enforcement of the segregation laws was harsh and vigorous, often involving savage beatings and expulsions from railway and street cars. Blacks suffered excessive force by state police forces and injustice in the courts. "In communities across the South, blacks came to perceive the law and its enforcers as an outside and alien force, an intrusive and repressive agency against which appeals for fairness and impartiality, humane and just treatment, were all but useless."[12]

9. Du Bois, *The Souls of Black Folk*, 1315.

10. Ibid., 1605; 1549.

11. Litwack, *Trouble in Mind*, 121.

12. Ibid., 277.

The Blues and Injustice

Charlie Patton reflected on the wretched conditions and situation of his people in "Down the Dirt Road Blues":

> Everyday seems like murder here,
> Everyday seems like murder here
> I'm gonna leave tomorrow
> I know you don't want me here.

Even having enough food to eat could not be taken for granted—Big Bill Broonzy in "I Can't Be Satisfied" sings, "Starvation in my kitchen, Rent sign's on my do."

Nor could either decent or, in some cases, any accommodation be taken for granted—as reflected poignantly by Blind Willie McTell's "Death Room Blues":

> Since my mother died and left me all alone,
> All my friends have forsaken me
> People I haven't even got a home.

And sometimes, things were just so bad that death seemed a better option. Consider Mississippi John Hurt's "Blue Harvest Blues":

> I'm just an orphan, where my folks is I don't know,
> With my heavy burden, Lord,
> I wished I was dead.

We have already noted briefly the injustice of the criminal justice system for the black population. We don't normally expect prisons to be a feature of musical history. But with the blues, it's not just drinkers, ramblers, and vagrants who take a starring role, but also convicts. The blues grew up not only in plantations but in prisons.

Parchman Farm was both a prison and plantation, extending over 20,000 acres of fertile Delta land, where prisoners were put to work as if they were slaves.[13] Prisoners were money-makers for the prison officials and the second greatest source of income for the state of Mississippi. Men worked until they dropped dead or burnt out with sunstroke. They worked from dawn to dusk in the brutal heat, surviving on worm-infested food, kept at it by the brutal application of the "Black Annie," a heavy leather strap. Bluesman Willie Dixon, who was born in 1915, was once sentenced

---

13. Giola, *Delta Blues*, 85

to thirty days for vagrancy on the Harvey Allen County Farm. He recalls the use of the Black Annie:

> They'd haul us out there to work and put us on a great big ditch. . . . We were on top cutting and all of a sudden I hear somebody screaming, "Oh Lawdy! Oh, Lawdy, captain please stop doing it."
> . . . I run over there peepin'. Boy, they've got five guys on this one guy . . . and this guy—they called him Captain Crush—has got a strap about eight inches wide. It's leather, about five or six inches long, a handle on it about two feet long and holes in the end of this strap about as big as a quarter, They called it the Black Annie.
> . . . Every time he hits this guy, flesh and blood actually come off this cat. . . . He was out and they were still beating him.[14]

Dixon goes on to relate how, for being caught watching this, he too was beaten with the strap round the head, resulting in deafness for the next four months. He was thirteen at the time.

But in these prison farms, remarkably, music thrived—mostly as a survival mechanism. When father and son musicologist team John and Alan Lomax set out on their famous blues-collecting road trip in 1933, they discovered that prisons were a great storehouse of music. They described finding here a "black Homer," an aging black prisoner called "Iron Head," with a songbook that would fill 500 pages if written down. They also found Huddie Ledbetter, later to be known as Leadbelly.

Possibly Leadbelly's most famous song is "Midnight Special," covered by Creedence Clearwater Revival, Van Morrison, and many others. The Midnight Special was a train whose headlights lit up Ledbetter's cell. The songs speaks of "Nothing in the pan," in other words nothing to eat, and if you were to "say a thing about it, you'd have trouble with the man." The song highlights the minor infractions that could put you away in a prison farm—"if you ever go the Houston, boy you'd better walk right. . . . Benson Crocker will arrest you, Jimmy Boone will take you down." Blacks often did not have to commit any crime in order to be arrested and subsequently jailed. A white person was completely at liberty to stop and question a black stranger in the neighborhood, and if the black did not have a local white person to vouch for him, then the police could be called upon to make an arrest. At one point, signs could be seen as you travelled south on the

---

14. Dixon with Snowden, *I Am the Blues*, 26.

railroad to New Orleans, saying things like "Nigger—Read and Run" or "Niggers and Dogs Not Allowed."[15]

Mattie May Thomas was a woman inmate at Parchman and the recording of her unaccompanied song tells her own sad tale:

> My knee bone hurt me and my ankles swell
> Yes I may get better, but I won't get well.
> There Mattie had a baby and he got blue eyes.
> They must be the captain, he keep a-hanging around
> . . . Six months ain't no sentence, baby, nine years ain't no time
> I got a buddy in the big house done from fourteen to twenty-nine.
> Ah the jailhouse was my beginning and the penitentiary's near my end
> And the electric chair is too big for me here.

Even by the standard of blues lyrics, these are unsettling words. But you get the same sense from most of the blues songs the Lomaxes recorded at Parchman—prisoners recounting personal tragedies, injustices, and the ever-present hope of pardon and freedom. Other famous blues convicts include Son House and Bukka White, second cousin to B. B. King. In his "Parchman Farm Blues," Bukka sings of the dawn-to-dusk work regime:

> Go to work in the mornin' just at the dawn of day
> And at the settin' of the sun that is when your work is done.

No wonder he also wrote "Fixin' to Die" blues:

> Now, I believe I'm fixin' to die, yeah
> I know I was born to die
> But I hate to leave my children around cryin'
> Yeah.

Although the blues are often songs about romantic loss, failure, or desire, and although they were undoubtedly designed for entertainment, there can be no doubting that it is the experience of suffering, hardship, the threat of violence, and, ultimately, injustice that provided the context and the catalyst for the blues. In all their varied reflections of struggle, discrimination, imprisonment, violence and poverty, blues songs tell the truth about the injustice of the world.

15. Litwack, *Trouble in Mind*, 239.

Justice—A Central Biblical Theme

A couple of years ago, I was at a weekend guitar workshop with my good friend Ken, and he started telling everybody about a blues night we had put on at my church a few months earlier. And everybody, to a man (yes, sadly, it was all men!), raised their eyebrows and said—What? Blues in a church? Come on! Which is a pretty standard reaction on both sides actually. Everybody wonders what the blues have to do with Christianity. Right from the start, many people thought of the blues as the devil's music. It's for outside of church, and we only sing hymns in here.

But once we start talking about the subject of justice, we begin to see that the blues and the church are not so far apart after all. Justice begins, firstly, with truth-telling and for sure the blues have always been about telling the truth about injustice in the world.

The Bible too is a truth-teller. It never shirks from the grim reality of life—as we read through its ancient texts, we read about war, rape, incest, slavery, abuse, people putting nails into other people's heads, crucifixion, murder, theft, and exploitation of the poor. All of human experience, all the suffering, all the injustice is right there.

And people like the ancient Jewish prophets, people like Amos and Micah and Isaiah, all saw it as their job to confront the regimes and the people of their day with the scandal of the injustice of exploitation of the poor. They railed against the ripping open of pregnant women in war, the trampling of the heads of the poor into the dust, against institutional injustice and those who were content to play music, drink wine, and anoint themselves with expensive oil while their fellow countrymen were ruined. The prophets were truth-tellers.

But here's the thing. In the middle of all this, this grim reality, there is an overall, overarching story of hope. The Bible has been much used and abused through the years, but the reality is that it has a basic, overarching narrative about God putting things right—in people, in his world. If anything might be said to be the major theme of Scripture, it is the idea of justice—God setting God's world right.

In a recent major work on the theme of justice, philosopher and theologian Nicholas Wolterstorff examines the prominence of this theme both the Old and New Testaments. In the Old Testament, he finds "the bottom ones, the low ones, the lowly," those at the wrong end of the social hierarchy, to be given a great deal of attention. Wolterstorff says,

> The prophets and the psalmist do not argue the case that alleviating the plight of the lowly is required by justice. They assume it. When they speak of God's justice, when they enjoin their hearers to practice justice, when they complain to God about the absence of justice, they take for granted that justice requires alleviating the plight of the lowly. They save their breath for urging their readers to actually practice justice to the . . . vulnerable low ones.[16]

Walter Brueggemann's assessment of the Old Testament is that "in Israel's core texts related to the Mosaic revolution, Yahwism is a practice of distributive justice."[17] Wolterstorff suggests that the Old Testament writers believed that widows, orphans, resident aliens, and the poor were disproportionately victims of injustice and that they understood the requirements of their God very well—to seek justice, to put things right, to undo injustice. He says bluntly: "Israel's religion was a religion of salvation, not of contemplation . . . not a religion of salvation *from this earthly existence* but a religion of salvation *from injustice* in this earthly existence."[18]

Wolterstorff's view of the prominence of this theme of justice and God wanting to put things right in the Old Testament is borne out by another comprehensive study of justice in the Bible by Enrique Nardoni. Nardoni's quite exhaustive study of all the literature in the Old Testament finds that it speaks of

> The active presence of the creative God in history, jealous of his sovereignty over the universe, and committed to exercising his liberating justice on behalf of an oppressed humanity.[19]

The Old Testament reveals a God whose rule is based on justice (Ps 89:14); who wants to "loose the bonds of injustice, to undo the thongs of the yoke, to let the oppressed go free, and to break every yoke" (Isa 58:6); who wants God's people to "share your bread with the hungry, and bring the homeless poor into your house; when you see the naked, to cover them" (Isa 58:7); who wants to establish a new world that God will uphold with justice (Isa 9:7), a world of peace, where even "the wolf and the lamb shall feed together" (Isa 65:25).

---

16. Wolterstorff, *Justice*, 76.

17. Brueggemann, *Theology of the Old Testament*, 738.

18. Wolterstorff, *Justice*, 79.

19. Nardoni, *Rise Up, O Judge*, 62.

The overarching narrative that we can detect in the Old Testament starts with a perfect world created by God, which has gone terribly wrong and is in the grip of evil and injustice. God then chooses a group of people through whom God will rectify the situation and put things right in God's world. We can see God doing this through calling Abraham and then by making a covenant at Sinai with the Hebrew ex-slaves God had liberated from Egypt. The rest of the Old Testament is largely the story of this people's struggle and failure to be the people of God in such a way that God's promises to Abraham would be fulfilled—that all the nations of the world would be blessed through this family. The story of Israel's failure to live up to its calling comes to its sad climax in the destruction of Jerusalem and the exile to Babylon in 587 BC. But right through the unfolding story, in the history books, the prophets, and the wisdom literature, we find glimpses of an understanding of the sort of world that Israel's God wants—a world of justice and equity, of peace and harmony. In fact, of course, in the literature of Israel's prophets we get much more than glimpses—the prophets were unstinting in their criticism of injustice perpetrated by the rich and powerful and consistent in their insistence on the requirements of Israel's God for both justice and compassion—especially towards those at the bottom, the poor and the oppressed. Nardoni points out that the prophets expected God to work in God's world and to bring about change through human beings. That being the case, there is

> A strong encouragement and an urgent invitation—encouragement both to those who suffer abuses and injustices and to those who work to correct them, and an invitation for people to participate in the implementation of God's plan.[20]

The revelation of God's purpose to bring justice to the world and to put things right carries on into the New Testament where we find God's son, the man Jesus, taking on himself all the injustice of the world, himself the victim of injustice, exhausting it and, by his resurrection, holding out the hope for God's final day of justice to come.

The story of the Bible is, yes, a *world gone wrong*—but it's also of a God who wants to fix things, to fix people, to fix their relationships and to fix the very fabric of his world.

When Jesus was on earth, he preached what he called the kingdom of God. That was not some other worldly, inner spiritual thing. This was

20. Ibid., 117.

rather a thoroughly Jewish idea, derived from Israel's scriptures, that Israel's God would return and rescue his people, and bring in a new day of peace, security, and justice. For Jesus, that day was arriving in and through his own person and ministry. So he began his preaching ministry in Mark 1:17 by telling people it was time to reorient their lives because the "kingdom of God was near." His whole ministry revolved around this message, this proclamation that God was coming to reclaim his world and that God was doing it through him, Jesus. And this new day of God's kingdom was to be a day of peace and justice—and so we hear him saying in the Sermon on the Mount, "Blessed are those who hunger and thirst after justice, for they shall be filled," and warning his followers that those who sought justice in this world would be persecuted.

The Greek word I've translated in Matthew 5 as "justice" is often rendered in Bible translations as "righteousness."[21] The word can be translated either way, but it is best to realize that the root idea behind the English word "righteousness" is one of justice—it's the state of things having been put right. Unfortunately the word has come to support a whole religious and theological infrastructure and its meaning has been somewhat obscured. So actually, "justice" does a better job in translating the word in our New Testaments. In Matthew 5:10 Jesus talks about being persecuted—have you ever heard of anyone being persecuted because of "righteousness"? Probably not, but on the other hand, it's commonplace to hear of people being harassed, victimized, and persecuted because of their pursuit of justice. Once you begin to stand out from the crowd and question the status quo, question the vested interests, you can be sure that persecution will follow.

So, what Jesus believed in and preached and demonstrated was that God wants to bring in a new day of justice, peace, and harmony. For Jesus, as a Jew, steeped in his scriptures, this was an expectation not that God was going to create some celestial city to which the redeemed would one day be taken, but rather that right here on earth, God would bring a new day of peace and justice. And this was not something that Jesus's followers were to passively sit around and wait for; no, they were to "hunger and thirst for"—actively, zealously, wholeheartedly pursue—justice right here and now. This, whatever the cost, would bring true happiness.

---

21. Hagner, *Matthew 1–13*, 6: "That δικαιοσύνη here means justice rather than 'personal righteousness,' is clear from the context. The poor, the grieving, and the downtrodden (i.e., those who have experienced injustice) are by definition those who long for God to act."

And then there is the teaching of Jesus in Matthew 25, where Jesus paints a picture of the final great assize, where God judges everyone. And the basis of his judgment is not a person's position or wealth, not the correctness of his or her theology, but rather whether he or she fed the hungry, welcomed the stranger, clothed the destitute, or visited the sick and those in prison. It's pretty stark, hard to wriggle out of. God the judge calls those who did all these things "the just." In the end, the question is, did we collaborate with God's grand justice-bringing, world-transforming project, or not?

And if we skip ahead in our New Testament a bit more, we find that the message of the Apostle Paul is basically the same as Jesus'. Like the other first Christians, Paul believed that the resurrection of Jesus had changed things fundamentally. This was God's stamp of vindication on Jesus; this was the beginning—the firstfruits (1 Cor 15:20), Paul calls it, of God's final resurrection; this was the beginning of a "new creation" (2 Cor 5:17), a new world that the resurrection of Jesus guarantees.

Paul, like Jesus, was convinced that God was going to come and bring in a new day of blessing and justice. That being the case, the imperative is for Jesus followers to live in the light of this coming justice. Paul says simply in his letter to the Roman Christians, "the kingdom of God . . . is justice, joy and peace in the Holy Spirit" (Rom 14:17). Christians are to live lives that reflect being "slaves of justice" (Rom 6:18) To live lives that proclaim justice, that seek justice; lives that tell the truth about the reality of the injustice in the world, and proclaim the hope of a new day.

And of course the Bible ends with that mysterious and terribly abused book of John's Revelation, which was written in the first century AD to tell the truth about the violent, oppressive regime of Rome, and also to hold out the hope that in the end, after all the violence and oppression of tyrants has been exhausted, God will have the last say, and there will indeed be a new day of peace and justice. In Revelation 19:8, at the culmination of all things, the pure white linen worn by the saints is said to be their "deeds of justice." Somehow at the end all the pursuing of justice, all the just deeds, all the ways in which we have looked after the poor and the oppressed, will be rolled up and taken up into the new world which God makes.

Despite the ways in which Christians have at times grievously misunderstood their faith and made it into either a system of oppressive power or of privatized spirituality, there are many examples of Christians throughout history who, out of their faith in a God of justice, have championed the cause of the poor, opposing forces of violence and oppression. One thinks of Francis of Assisi, who opposed the wealth and affluence of the church at the turn of the thirteenth century, opposed the Crusades, and welcomed in both poor and outcast. Or Archbishop Desmond Tutu in our own day, who highlighted to the world the evil of apartheid and saw it as his Christian duty and service to oppose the oppressive regime in his country. We could add to these, of course, names like William Wilberforce, Elizabeth Fry, Martin Luther King Jr., Mother Teresa, and many, many more examples. The list is almost endless.

Injustice and Truth-Telling

A sense of justice is something that I think we all feel quite deeply about. We all want things to be right, to be fair—this is something we have from when we were children. Do you remember when the teacher decided to punish the whole class because one person did something wrong and wouldn't own up? So *everybody* had to stay late! We felt deep down—that's not fair; I didn't do it; don't punish me as well! Or when you had to go to bed before your big brother or sister—boy, didn't that just seem wrong—why should he get to see that football match when I can't? "It's so unfair!"

And as we get older, the issues change, but our sense of fairness, of wanting things to be right, stays with us. And we begin to realize that while sometimes we suffer some unfairness in our own lives, there's an awful lot of unfairness out there in the world.

Bob Dylan's 1993 song, "World Gone Wrong" points to the disastrous state of the world:

> Feel bad this morning, ain't got no home,
> No use in worrying, 'cause the world gone wrong
> I can't be good baby
> Honey because the world gone wrong.

The song's primarily about a personal world that's gone wrong, but it hits the right note of despair about the way things are in the world. Whether personal or global, the world's gone wrong and we feel there's nothing we can do about it.

That the world's gone wrong, there's no doubt—we've watched the economies of the major Western nations tank, ripped off by banking greed and recklessness; we've seen riots in the streets of major European cities as people react with anger to the helplessness they feel about what's happening.

Our safe developed world no longer seems so safe; and, of course, it's the case that, despite our economic woes, we are still a small minority floating on a huge sea of poverty and need in two-thirds of the world.

Poverty, hunger, preventable sickness and war, corruption, and unfair trade rules are causing terrible suffering—we see but a fraction of the reality on our TV screens each night. Hundreds of millions of people in our world don't get the chance to make a living, feed themselves, send their kids to school, or create a better future for the next generation. So there's no doubt—the world's gone wrong. Injustice is built into the very fabric of the way the world works.

If injustice is going to be put right, the first thing that needs to be done is for the truth to be told. Our Western society does everything in its power—with technology, with advertising, with entertainment—to lull us into a false sense that everything's okay, that we're okay and so the world's okay. We're bombarded with media all day long so that our minds are dulled and our consciences dampened. The truth is, however, that our world is out of sync.

And it's here, I think, that the blues, over the past ninety years, has been a voice crying in the wilderness. In the midst of a world in denial, the blues tells the truth. Because the blues speaks of the real-world suffering and hardship of real people.

There's a very interesting recent example of the blues standing up to injustice and bringing hope—and, interestingly, joining forces with the church as well. During the 1980s, while communist regimes still held the Eastern part of Europe in their grip, there was a protest movement that grew up in East Berlin. Blues musician Günter Holly Holwas and church minister Rainer Eppelmann initiated what came to be known as the blues mass. Radio Free Europe reported that "the first blues mass in July 1979 attracted more than 300 people and was a roaring success. These blues masses offered what East Germany's youth had been craving: good live music and unfettered debates on social and political issues, along with a touch of spirituality through religious services. They instantly grew into a major dissident platform that many believe paved the way for the DDR's demise."[22] I contacted Holly Holwas recently and he told me that the secret police watched him twenty-four hours a day for three years—and when

22. http://www.rferl.org/content/In_OnceDivided_City_East_Berliners_Still_See_Us_And_Them_/1870974.html

East German authorities finally succeeded in crushing the blues masses in 1986, they were drawing almost 10,000 people from all over the DDR.

So maybe the idea of blues in a church isn't so strange after all. Both the church and the blues are forthright about the way the world is—it's a world gone wrong; it's a world full of injustice. And neither the Christian gospel nor the blues let us just be numbed by popular culture into thinking that everything's okay. Because everything is not okay.

And both the blues, in its own way, and Christian faith, in its very essence, point to the hope of a better world ahead, a world of love, a world of fairness, a world of satisfied minds, a world where injustice is a thing of the past. W. E. B. Du Bois said, "Through all the sorrow songs there breathes a hope—a faith in the ultimate justice of things."[23] A common theme, then, in our Christian faith and in the blues is this theme of justice—telling the stark truth about the way things are and looking for a better future, based on fairness and what's right.

Listening Guide

Bob Dylan, *World Gone Wrong*, Sony, 1997

Blind Willie McTell, *Blues Masters: Blind Willie McTell*, Music For Jazz Aficionados, 2012

Big Bill Broonzy, *Trouble in Mind*, Smithsonian Folkways, 2009.

Also, check out this great tribute album to Bill Broonzy: Billy Boy Arnold, *Sings Big Bill Broonzy*, Electro-Fi, 2012

Charlie Patton, *The Best of*, Shanachie Entertainment, 2005

23. Du Bois, *The Souls of Black Folk*, 189.

four

Violence, the Blues, and Peace

Blessed are the peacemakers,
for they will be called children of God.

MATTHEW 5:9

A Hollow Victory in Winning

Texas blueswoman Carolyn Wonderland typically sings with great passion and power, and she's an outstanding blues guitarist to boot. She's also a peace activist and is known for her fund-raising for local charities —food banks, soup kitchens, homeless shelters—in Austin, where she lives. On her 2011 album, *Peace Meal*, the track "Only God Knows When" is a powerful song about peace. The first verse has the great line "violence is no solution when life ain't like you planned," which Wonderland tells us applies to individuals and nations alike. Despite the appetite for war we've seen over the past ten years in the US and the UK, "There's a hollow victory in winning, when everybody pays the cost, With retaliations by the hour, lives and generations lost."

One thinks of the indiscriminate violence against civilians and children in Fallujah in 2004, which resulted in thousands of deaths and untold suffering to many more; or the planet's deadliest conflict since World War II in the Democratic Republic of Congo, which has claimed the lives of an estimated 5.4 million people, 50 percent of whom have been children, and has seen hundreds of thousands of women and girls raped; or the conflict that has raged in Darfur in the Sudan, where two million people have died as a result of war, famine, and disease, and four million people have been displaced at least once (and often repeatedly) during the war.

The problem is, of course, everybody thinks they're in the right and, often, that they've got God on their side. "Everybody thinks that they're righteous, or they never even would have fought," sings Wonderland—or as acoustic bluesman Eric Bibb put it in his song "Got to Do Better," "Hatred's a luxury, the price is too high." Too often war is not the last resort and the cost—which is usually in the lives of innocent women and children—is not properly counted.

It's strange how quickly Christians have been, all too often, willing or even keen to support military actions. Particularly when you remember that Jesus's birth was announced by the shepherds as heralding "peace on earth"; when he said things like "love your enemies" and "blessed are those who make peace"; and when he offered no resistance to his torturers prior to his execution. Jesus's good news proclamation was that the kingdom of God was arriving through his own life. This was the same good news that the biblical prophet Isaiah talked about, and the good news was that as a result of God coming to reign, there would be peace (Isa 52:7). There would come a day when wolves and lambs would graze together (Isa 65:25) and children wouldn't be "born to a world of horrors" (Isa 65:23).

The word "peace" occurs more than 100 times in the New Testament and at our peril we relegate this to some notion of "inner peace." More often than not it's about God wanting peace among God's creatures. In St. Paul's Letter to the Romans, he says (chapter 12) that Christians are never to take vengeance, should live in harmony with one another, should bless those who persecute them, should serve and help their enemies, repay no one evil for evil, and live peaceably with all. Not much wiggle room there then, is there? Peace was central to Jesus's mission and that of the first Christians— it ought to be just as crucial for modern Jesus followers.

As Willard Swartley contends in his book *Covenant of Peace*, the "New Testament consistently not only supports nonviolence but also advocates proactive peacemaking, consisting of positive initiatives to overcome evil, employing peaceable means to make peace."[1]

---

1. Swartley, *Covenant of Peace*, xi.

Jesus and Peacemaking

One of Jesus's sayings recorded for us by Matthew in the Sermon on the Mount is "Blessed are the peacemakers, for they will be called children of God." He goes on to intensify the force of the fifth commandment of the Decalogue—"do not commit murder"—so that anger against another is brought into the frame:

> You have heard that it was said to those of ancient times, "You shall not murder"; and "whoever murders shall be liable to judgment." But I say to you that if you are angry with a brother or sister, you will be liable to judgment; and if you insult a brother or sister, you will be liable to the council; and if you say, "You fool," you will be liable to the hell of fire. (Matt 5:21–22)

Furthermore, Jesus says that his followers are to love their enemies and pray for those who harass them; they are to "turn the other cheek, when slapped"; and, in a situation of being occupied by a pagan foreign power, they were to carry the oppressor's bag twice as far as might normally be required.

Genuine love is to be shown to everyone, explains Jesus, not just to those who love us. He sums up his teaching at the end of chapter 5 by saying:

> Be perfect, therefore, as your heavenly Father is perfect [in show-ing love to everyone] (Matt 5:48).

It all sounds like a tall order, doesn't it, when there are so many "bad guys" out there, terrorists "who want to take away our freedom," and all sorts of people who seek to oppose us and frustrate us in our everyday lives? Is peace a realistic option?

Often when we talk about peace, we are really most concerned about *our* peace—how often do you hear the phrase "peace with security," which is really just a justification of using violence and military force to secure our own well-being, our own political and economic prosperity, no matter what the cost to others (the "collateral damage"). All too often Christians, as much as anybody else, buy into a nationalistic definition of peace which enables an accommodation of the use of lethal military force for "maintain-ing our way of life."

In a discussion of Ephesians 2:11–22, where Paul talks about Christ being our "peace" and having made peace between two groups that hated each other, Thomas Yoder Neufeld says,

> This text reminds us that there is no evangelical and missional way
> of speaking of Christ that does not come to terms with the radical
> spiritual, social, and even cosmic dimensions of peace.

He goes on to say that Paul's words mean that it is "inconceivable that one could come to know the peace of God without being drawn in to the costly making of peace in our world."[2]

We have seen already that the central theme in Jesus's preaching was the kingship or rule of God. The good news or gospel that he preached was essentially the same gospel preached by the prophet Isaiah, who looked forward to the dawning of the new day of God's just and peaceful reign on the earth. The essence of Isaiah's gospel is found in chapter 52:7:

> How beautiful upon the mountains are the feet of the messenger
> Who announces peace
> Who brings good news
> Who announces salvation,
> Who says to Zion, "Your God reigns."

The essence of the good news proclaimed by the messenger is that "God reigns" and clearly the result of that is both salvation and peace. Isaiah raises the expectation for God's people, in their experience of exile and loss, for a new exodus, a new day of joy, peace, and glory.[3]

The term "kingdom of God" is rarely found in the Old Testament, yet the idea of Yahweh as king is pervasive—found in the Pentateuch, the history books, the Psalms, and the Prophets. And the blessing of God's reign was characterized by the Hebrew word *shalom*, which occurs some 235 times in the Old Testament. The word has a broad meaning, encompassing well-being, safety, security, health, and prosperity. It clearly includes the idea of absence of war, but it is much wider than that. Leviticus 26:6 simply says that Yahweh "will grant peace (shalom) in the land," with the indication that shalom is the correlate of Yahweh's presence. It is the state of affairs that accompanies justice, as is indicated by Psalm 85:10—"Love and truth will meet; justice and peace will kiss," when Yahweh brings salvation to his people. In Psalm 29, which proclaims Yahweh as "enthroned as King forever," the blessing of Yahweh to his people is said to be shalom (v. 11).

The prophets began to talk about an heir of David who would bring a new era of shalom (Isa 9:1–7)—in fact this one would be the "Prince of

---

2. Yoder Neufeld, "For he is our peace: Ephesians 2:11–22," 229–30.

3. Mauser, *The Gospel of Peace*, 25.

Peace." Two chapters further on, Isaiah describes this era as one of justice, freedom from enemies, protection from wild animals, freedom from suffering, and harmony between peoples.

The Greek word for peace is *eirene*, which predominantly had the sense of absence of war. Yet this is the word that the translators of the Greek Bible (LXX), which was used by the first Christians, used to translate the Hebrew *shalom*. Mauser suggests that "In the New Testament . . . it is quite manifest that *eirene* is used in meanings far transcending the traditional narrow connotation in pre-Hellenistic Greek, preserving important aspects of the range of significations."[4] So, given that the New Testament writers were all Jewish and readers of the LXX, we might confidently expect that when we read the word *eirene*, which is translated in our English New Testaments as "peace," the word reflects the broad Jewish sense of shalom, the idea of well-being which is the result of Yahweh reigning in the world.

In Acts 10:36, Peter proclaims that the message from God which came through Jesus Christ was "the good news of peace." Perhaps we shouldn't be surprised at this, since God is so often described in the New Testament as the "God of peace."[5]

The message of peace is the message that because of Jesus the Messiah, God has broken into the world in a new way to bring in a new day of shalom. The gospel is the good news that the shalom—the wholeness, well-being, and peace—envisaged by God's people in the Old Testament as accompanying the arrival of God's rule, has, in fact, arrived because of the life, death, and resurrection of Jesus.

We really cannot separate the idea of peace from the gospel. Nor will it do to confine the notion of peace to either simply the idea of individual, spiritual peace with God or some sort of personal, inner, psychological peace as a result of faith. The idea of shalom will simply not let us get away with that. The challenge for us here is to expand our idea of the enormous scope of the Christian gospel to see that it has ramifications for every part of human life and that the peace of the gospel has much wider implications than our own inner sense of forgiveness and calm. And also that, although the biblical idea of peace or shalom is a broad one, we certainly cannot get away from the sense of peace as absence of war or violence.

---

4. Ibid., 29.

5. Rom 15:33; 16:20; 1 Cor 14:33; 2 Cor 13:11; Phil 4:9; 1 Thess 5:23; 2 Thess 3:16; Heb 13:20.

In John's gospel, at his trial, Jesus tells the Roman governor Pilate that "my kingdom is not of this world," which is often interpreted as meaning that Jesus was reassuring Pilate that he had nothing to fear from his followers because the kingdom they were concerned about was internal and spiritual—"in their hearts." And yet, after this statement, Jesus immediately follows up by saying that "if it were, my followers would have taken up arms," indicating that what Jesus was actually saying was, in effect, "my kingdom is not the same as yours, Pilate. Violence and force is not the way that my kingdom works. It's different in its very essence." The point is not physical versus spiritual—it is violence versus peace. Jesus's kingdom simply did not work in the same way as the Roman Empire, which established its rule by violence and maintained it by the threat of violence. Nor does it work in the same way as any other system of violence and military force—it is, in its very essence, a peaceful kingdom.

We have become so used to the rhetoric of violence in our modern world that it has become very hard to hear the message of Jesus—as Peter said, it is the good news of *peace*.

So, returning to Jesus's words in the Sermon, as Swartley points out:

> The Beatitudes, in all their beauty, are really about God's sustaining presence for lowly people as they experience difficulties and encounter obstacles. They mark out the fundamental nature of life in the kingdom of God.[6]

The blessings of which the Beatitudes speak refer to the experience of God's grace for those who recognize and seek to live under the rule of the messianic kingdom herald, Jesus. The promise to those who are peacemakers—who seek to actualize the shalom that is the hallmark of this new revolutionary kingdom—is that they will be recognized as God's children. This is because, in their peacemaking, they reflect the very nature of God himself—they show the family resemblance, so much is peace a part of God. God is, as we have seen, the God of peace.

Then and now, peacemaking was a tall order. We live in a world where violence is part of the fabric of life—as it was in Jesus's day. Yet it is the very thing that is to identify Jesus's followers—peacemaking distinguishes them as God's children. And Jesus proceeds then to further define this peacemaking—it includes the unthinkable task of loving enemies. Jesus intensifies

---

6. Swartley, *Covenant of Peace*, 54.

the Jewish law's requirement to love our neighbors by saying, "But I say to you, love your enemies and pray for those who harass you."

Matthew clearly didn't feel this saying of Jesus's was an impossible ideal—he was writing at least fifty years after the death of Jesus and highlighted the church's mission as making disciples of all nations (Matt 28:19), which presumably included passing along Jesus's teaching about nonviolent love of enemies. And, clearly, this was something that Jesus himself practiced, right through to his capture, torture, and violent death. This is a command from Jesus, then, that we need to take seriously.

Jesus's teaching in Matthew 5:39ff., which includes turning the other cheek, giving your last item of clothing to someone who is suing you, going the extra mile, lending freely, and praying for your enemies, speaks of the generosity and peace-loving way of life that is to characterize his followers. As Richard Hays points out, however, this is not simply "supine passivity." Rather,

> By doing more than what the oppressor requires, the disciples bear witness to another reality (the kingdom of God), a reality in which peacefulness, service and generosity are valued above self-defense and personal rights.[7]

Jesus concludes this section of the Sermon with the words, "Therefore, just as your heavenly Father is complete in showing love to everyone, so also you must be complete." Our peacemaking, love of enemies, and nonviolent response to harassment enables us to show God's character to the world—it witnesses to the reality of the alternative kingdom that Jesus spoke to Pilate about. There is a power at work in the world that is greater than that of naked force—it is the power of love. There is a different way of being human than one which promotes, or desperately tries to protect, our own interests—it's what Paul calls the "new creation," the new reality that God has inaugurated in the world through Christ.

The problem is that we are too conditioned by the way things are to really believe that things could be different. And the New Testament's message of peacemaking and love of enemies has become as incredible to us as it is to everyone else. As Hays puts it, on this point the church has become "massively faithless."[8] He goes on to say that,

---

7. Hays, *The Moral Vision of the New Testament*, 326.

8. Ibid., 343.

> only when the church renounces the way of violence, will people see what the Gospel means. . . . The meaning of the New Testament's teaching on violence will become evident only in communities of Jesus's followers who embody the costly way of peace.

No Shalom Here

Black Americans in the Southern states in the early decades of the twentieth century, during which time the blues emerged, did not experience much shalom. There was little well-being, security, or wholeness about their lives. Black neighborhoods typically were poor environments, unpaved, without sewage facilities, deteriorating, and disease-ridden. Housing conditions were appalling—"hardly more than rickety shacks clustered on stilts like Daddy Long Legs along the slimy bank of putrid and evil smelling 'Cripple Creek.'"[9] W. E. B. Du Bois said that the Atlanta black population suffered "bad health, poor family life, and crime" as a direct result of living conditions, and that "the high death rate of the Negro is directly traceable to these slum districts."[10] Preventable diseases such as tuberculosis, typhoid, and diarrhea were rife in black areas due to undernourishment, ignorance, and poverty.[11] In 1900 in Atlanta, 45 percent of black children died before their first birthday.[12] Such conditions were typical across the South during this period. Life was hard and uncertain, and suffering was virtually guaranteed. The blues, then, emerged as one response to the deprivation and suffering of a people.

Take, for example, "T.B.'s Killing Me," recorded by Georgia bluesman Buddy Moss in 1933:

> I went to the doctor of the sea
> I sat right down and he looked at me
> He said I hate to tell you but you got disease
> You ain't got nothing but them old TBs
> Oh TB is killing me . . .
>
> . . . And it won't be long before some lonely graveyard I'll be.

9. Robinson, *Road Without Turning*, 18.

10. Galishoff, "Germs Know No Color Line," 22–41. Du Bois is quoted from his *The American Negro*, 60.

11. Litwack, *Trouble in Mind*, 337.

12. Galishoff, "Germs Know No Color Line," 23.

Before this Victoria Spivey had recorded "T.B. Blues" in 1927 and then "Dirty T.B. Blues" in 1929. She followed it up with another TB song in 1936, "T.B.'s Got Me." Clearly, this disease, for which poverty is a determinant, was prevalent in black communities at the time.

It is often the case that oppressors proclaim peace when, actually, there is no peace for the people who are being oppressed. The prophet of ancient Israel, Jeremiah, berated the rulers of his nation for treating "the wound of my people as though it were not serious and for saying 'Peace, peace,' when there was no peace" (Jer 8:11). People, he said, were looking for peace, and for a time of healing, but there was "terror" instead (Jer 8:15). Move on a few centuries and the slogans of the Roman Empire for its conquered peoples were *pax* and *iustitia*—peace and justice. The propaganda of every violent regime or empire to its conquered peoples seems to be the same— it's a good thing that we're the ones in charge, our rule will bring you peace, our rules will make for proper justice. George W. Bush in 2001 promised that "peace and freedom" would prevail, as he led the US into a long and costly military action in Afghanistan. In the three months subsequent to this statement, it is reckoned that at least 4,200–4,500 Afghan civilians were killed as a result of the US war and air strikes.[13] In addition, as many as 20,000 innocent men, women, and children lost their lives as an indirect consequence of the US intervention.[14]

No matter how many times the propaganda is pumped out, those who suffer as "collateral damage" in war or who are in subjection know that proclamations of peace and well-being by empires or oppressors is a lie, and that for all these assertions, there is no experience of shalom for them.

We have already seen that in addition to more generalized conditions of poverty and discrimination, Southern blacks suffered abuse and violence from the white population, in terms of casual brutality, lynching, or po-groms. In Atlanta in 1906 there occurred what is often referred to as a "race riot," which in reality was a savage outburst of violence directed towards the black community by white people drawn from every class of society. During four days, much of Atlanta was destroyed by 10,000 white people burning and looting black areas, with the result that twenty-six people (just one white) were killed and 200 were seriously injured. The dead blacks were

---

13. Conetta, "Operation Enduring Freedom," Project on Defense Alternatives 13.

14. Steele, "Forgotten Victims."

found to be "honest, industrious, and law-abiding citizens" who had suffered "unspeakable brutality."[15]

The blues, then, developed in an environment of violence, and can be said to be a reaction to that violence. Charlie Patton reflected the constant threat of violent death in "Down the Dirt Road Blues,"

> Every day seems like murder here
> Every day seems like murder here
> I'm gonna leave tomorrow
> I know you don't want me here.

The terror that was ever present for black Americans in the Southern states in the early decades of the twentieth century, particularly with the threat of lynching or being sold into peonage, could not be met with either protest or self-defense. Resistance came in the form of both religion and the blues. Says Cone, "At the juke joints on Friday and Saturday nights and at churches on Sunday mornings and evening week nights blacks affirmed their humanity and fought back against dehumanization."[16]

Both faith and the blues enabled African Americans to resist their oppressors in nonviolent ways. Dancing, laughter, and self-expression in the juke joint enabled blacks for a few hours each week to escape the assault on their humanity from white society. The blues was "a disposition to confront the most unpromising circumstances and make the most of what little there is to go on, regardless of the odds."[17] For James Cone, the blues was a musical response "that told the world about the cultural power of blacks to preserve and protect their humanity."[18] Sometimes the response in the blues was refracted through songs about love and romantic problems, but sometimes it was more explicit. Take, for example, Maggie Jones's "Northbound Blues" from 1925, where the desire to get away to a freer, less oppressive environment is openly expressed:

> Going north child, where I can be free
> Where there's no hardships, like in Tennessee.

Cow Cow Davenport in his "Jim Crow Blues" gives us the same sentiment:

15. Litwack, *Trouble in Mind*, 316.

16. Cone, *The Cross and the Lynching Tree*, 14.

17. Murray, *Stomping the Blues*, 6.

18. Cone, *The Cross and the Lynching Tree*, 11.

> I'm tired of being Jim Crowed
> Gonna leave this Jim Crow town.

Or consider Leadbelly's "Jim Crow," where he appeals to his community to resist the oppression:

> Been traveling, I been traveling from shore to shore
> Everywhere I have been I find some old Jim Crow . . .
> Down in Louisiana, Tennessee, Georgia's a mighty good place to go
> And get together, break up this old Jim Crow.

The blues enabled Southern blacks to process the oppression they faced, but more than that, to affirm their humanity over against a system that denied that very fact. It enabled them to state the reality of their troubles, powerlessness, dread, and despair, but at the same time to assert their essential humanness through expressions of rage, humor, courage, and of course, sexuality.

Violence in the Juke

Having said that, we do have to reckon with the fact that in the places where the blues were regularly performed, the juke joints, there was a considerable amount of violence, black on black. "Wherever the blues is played," said Charles Love, ragtime jazzman, "there's a fight right after."[19] There can be no doubt that a great deal of "cutting and shooting" went on in the jukes. These could be very dangerous places. According to Stephen Calt and Gayle Wardlow, violence was widespread in country "frolics," where blues was played.[20] Memphis Minnie said that at juke joints she and her husband would "have to run at night when they start cutting and shooting." Minnie herself was not averse to resorting to violence—Johnny Shines recalled, "they tell me she shot one old man's arm off, or cut it with a hatchet . . . Minnie was a hellraiser, I know that!"[21]

The mixture of letting your hair down on a Saturday night after a long week of hard labor, freedom from white supervision, an abundance of alcohol, and the music itself was an explosive one. The violence of the juke is evident from many of the blues songs—Mississippi John Hurt's "Make Me a Pallet," which talks about his "good gal" who might turn up and catch his

---

19. Oliver, *Conversations with the Blues*, 81.
20. Calt and Wardlow, *King of the Delta Blues*, 61.
21. Garon and Garon, *Woman with Guitar*, 69–80, 77.

new lover to "cut and shoot" her; Little Walter's "Boom Boom, Out Goes the Light," where the singer says "I've been looking for my baby all night, If I get her in my sight . . . Boom Boom! Out goes the light"; a popular early blues number, "See See Rider 44," which says, "I'm gonna buy me a pistol, just as long as I am tall, Gonna kill my man and catch the Cannonball"—are just some examples.

Even as late as the sixties, there was violence associated with the blues. Paul Oscher was a white harmonica player for Muddy Waters for a while and recalls that everybody carried guns. He claimed that Muddy Waters always carried a .25 automatic and a .22 in his shirt pocket, not to mention the .38 in his car. Even with the band, "the only reason everybody didn't get killed was that everybody knew everybody else had a gun."[22] Mike Bloomfield, a white blues guitarist in the sixties, said that many times in the Chicago blues clubs he was scared—"I saw knifings and shootings. . . . It was a very violent scene, man."[23]

The blues, both in terms of the violent context in which they flourished, and in terms of the often violent environment in which they were played, can be said to be indicative of the lack of shalom experienced by the black communities under the oppression of Jim Crow.

Churches and Peace

And yet, as we have seen, peace is an essential element in the New Testament's gospel message. But when we come to consider the white churches' response to the lack of shalom experienced by the Southern black community under Jim Crow, sadly we largely find complicity in the hardship and oppression suffered by African Americans.

This has been too often the case with the church of Jesus Christ throughout history. While we can find plenty of examples of care, compassion, and the pursuit of justice by Christians, we also find a blindness to the requirements of the gospel with respect to peace, and a lack of understanding that God is the "God of peace." Where I grew up and live, in Northern Ireland, we have experienced social upheaval over the past forty years, which has only recently begun to settle down. While the conflict was essentially one of national identity rather than religion per se (are you British or Irish?), neither the Protestant nor the Roman Catholic churches (with

22. Tooze, *Muddy Waters*, 217–18.

23. Wolkin and Keenom, *Michael Bloomfield*, 28.

some wonderful, notable exceptions) managed to be true messengers of peace because of the close national associations that they were unwilling to forego. On the side of the fence I am most familiar with, Protestant Christians were often either ignorant of or unwilling to acknowledge genuine, historical grievances suffered by the Irish nationalist community, and too often associated with a defiant, unflinching "unionism" (ensuring Northern Ireland remained part of the United Kingdom). That said, the "peace process" that began in the 1990s and has brought an end to the "troubles" was largely initiated by exceptionally brave church leaders from both sides of the community. However, preaching peace, for the most part, was not for either side a major concern.

James Cone notes that lynchers in the Southern states were "good citizens" who considered themselves Christians. He also makes the point that during this period, white theologians, who developed a Christian social ethic during the early part of the twentieth century, seemed to be blind to the scandal of white supremacy. "Whites could claim a Christian identity from the horrendous violence committed against black people."[24] Cone points out the dark irony here, where lynchers were Christians who claimed to worship a man strung up in Jerusalem. He accuses white Christians of treating the cross of Jesus Christ as simply a symbol of abstract, sentimental piety, and ignoring its stark testimony to human suffering. "We are called," says Cone, "to more than contemplation and adoration" before the cross. We need "to take the crucified down from the cross."[25]

This reminds us of the parable of great assize in Matthew 25, where Jesus poses the question, "On what basis will God make his judgement on the last day?" Perhaps to the surprise of many of today's Christians, nowhere in his answer does he refer to belief, baptism, or theology. Instead, God's welcome at the last is for those who fed the hungry, looked after the homeless and the sick, and visited those in prison. The truth that is so uncomfortable to well-fed, consuming, and well-entertained Europeans and North Americans is that only those who are truly seeking the shalom of the world are the "sheep" whom God will welcome home.

The story of the black church, on the other hand, "is a tale of variety and struggle in the midst of constant racism and oppression."[26] As much as they could, church leaders protested the effects of Jim Crow laws and the

24. Cone, *The Cross and the Lynching Tree*, 159.

25. Ibid., 161; see also Sobrino, *No Salvation Outside the Poor*, 1–17.

26. Maffly-Kipp, "An Introduction to the Church in the Southern Black Community."

systematic violence of lynching, while many blacks viewed white Christianity as hypocrisy. Ida B. Wells, a former slave whom Du Bois called "the pioneer of the anti-lynching crusade," found courage and determination in her Christian faith and "challenged white liberal Christians to speak out against lynching or be condemned by their silence."[27] James Cone has branded Southern white Christianity during this period as "fraudulent," and says that "the Christian identity of whites was not a true expression of what it meant to follow Jesus."[28] The church provided a source of hope for black Christians during these dark days and a community in which there could be mutual support, comfort, and, wherever possible, protest. In John Perkins's autobiography, he says that, "Ever since slavery the black church in the South served as the only place where black people could get together and speak freely."[29]

There was within the black churches not only a personal element to Christian faith, but also a realization that there were, inherent in that faith, practical implications for equality, justice, and liberation. James Cone makes the link between that most potent and central of Christian symbols, the cross of Jesus Christ, and the suffering which it signifies, and the suffering of blacks under Jim Crow. He says simply, "If today . . . I cling to the old rugged cross, it is because I have seen with my own eyes how that symbol empowered black people to stand up and become agents of change for their freedom."[30]

In many ways, the civil rights movement, which resulted in the desegregation and reforms of the 1960s, had its roots in Christianity. Many of its leaders, both men and women, were Christians, including, of course, Dr. Martin Luther King Jr. This movement was in essence a movement of nonviolence. King eschewed "the advocacy of violence as a tool of advancement, organized as in warfare, deliberately and consciously," and championed a nonviolent noncooperation with evil. King did not believe in passivity, but rather in an active form of community resistance, which he believed ultimately would triumph, despite the suffering that it would inevitably entail. King knew the way of nonviolence may "not immediately change the heart of the oppressor. It first of all does something to the hearts

27. Du Bois, "Ida B. Wells-Barnett: Postscript," 207; Wells, "Our Country's Lynching Record," 280.

28. Cone, *The Cross and the Lynching Tree*, 132.

29. Perkins, *Let Justice Roll Down*, 54.

30. Cone, *The Cross and the Lynching Tree*, 132.

and souls of those committed to it. It gives them new self-respect; it calls up resources of strength and courage that they did not know they had. Finally, it reaches the opponent and so stirs his conscience that reconciliation becomes a reality."[31]

Faith, the Blues, and Peace

The nonviolent movement for civil rights that King led is just one of many campaigns where the weapon of nonviolent protest has proven stronger than the gun and tank. Examples abound, both in history and in the recent past, but so used are we to a response of violence that it often appears to be the only option.[32] The problem often is not that nonviolence is ineffective, but rather that it is so rarely countenanced as an option.

How is it that Christians have so readily made peace with war, given the biblical description of God as "the God of peace" and Jesus as "the prince of peace"? From Jesus's teaching in the Gospels right through the New Testament, peace is one of the prime characteristics of God's reign, which Christ inaugurated and which his followers are supposed to live in and express. The writer to the Hebrews puts it simply and straightforwardly—"pursue peace with everyone" (Heb 12:14).

We've seen that the peace that is the necessary accompaniment to God's reign is more than just absence of war—it is the shalom of the Old Testament, which speaks of wholeness, well-being, and human flourishing. As we look back over the history of the blues, we are confronted with a people who were subjected to injustice and oppression in such a way as to deny them such shalom. The blues was at once an expression of protest at the experience of violence and lack of shalom, and also a way of blacks seeking to claim their humanness in the face of terror and humiliation.

It is a cry from the heart against everything that mitigates against human flourishing and reminds us of the reality of human suffering and the negative effects of violence, for which the answer is life in the compassionate, peacemaking, and loving kingdom of God.

This is precisely the theme of the Rev. Gary Davis's simple but catchy song "Let us Get Together," which says,

---

31. King Jr., *I Have a Dream*, 60.

32. For an excellent summary of a range of successful nonviolent campaigns which led to real change and justice, see Gonzalez, *God's Reign and the End of Empires*, 309–12.

> Let us get together, Right down here . . .
> Let us walk together, Right down here . . .
> Let us do our living. Right down here.

And then reflects the prayer that Jesus taught his disciples, asking for God's kingdom to come, on earth, as it is in heaven:

> Let us have our heaven
> Right down here.

Recommended Listening

Carolyn Wonderland, *Peace Meal,* Bismeaux Productions, 2011

Various artists, *I Can't Be Satisfied: Early American Women Blues Singers, Vol. 2,* Shanachie Entertainment, 2005

Mississippi John Hurt, *Rediscovered,* Vanguard Records, 1998

Also see these two excellent tributes to this important blues artist:

Various artists, *Avalon Blues: A Tribute To The Music Of Mississippi John Hurt,* Vanguard Records, 2005

Rory Block, *Avalon: A Tribute To Mississippi John Hurt,* Stony Plain, 2013

Memphis Minnie, *When The Levee Breaks,* Goldenlane Records, 2010

Also see the tribute album to Memphis Minnie:

Maria Muldaur and various artists, *First Came Memphis Minnie,* Vivid Sound, 2012 *five*

There Must be a Better World Somewhere

Your kingdom come. Your will be done,
on earth as it is in heaven.

MATTHEW 6:10

A Prayer for Revolutionaries

In Matthew chapter 6, as part of the Sermon on the Mount, Jesus gives his followers a model prayer—which we now know as "the Lord's Prayer." Ever since then, Christians have been praying this prayer when they gather together, often as a matter of form—it's just part of the service, it's what you do, and it's often recited without any real understanding of its explosive, revolutionary nature.

But this prayer is indeed a prayer for revolutionaries. It is shot through with urgency and a desire for God to come and bring transformation to the world—"may your kingly rule come," Jesus prays, "let your purposes prevail here on earth, in the same way they do in your own heavenly realm." The prayer reflects Jesus's whole mission and passion—to see the peaceful, loving reign of God established here on earth. We've seen already how such ideas were part of the thinking and expectation of Jesus and his Jewish contemporaries in the early first century AD.

Jesus's teaching and actions must all be understood within this framework of the kingdom of God, the long-expected return of Israel's God to Zion to bring decisively a new day of shalom, forgiveness of sins, and joy.

What set Jesus apart from other groups of Jews who harbored such hopes and dreams was that he believed that God was doing this through himself. Jesus was encouraged by scriptural texts such as Daniel 7, which speaks of Israel's God offering "authority, glory and sovereign power" to "one like a son of man" such that "all nations and peoples of every language worshiped him," giving him "an everlasting dominion that will not pass away, and [a] kingdom . . . that will never be destroyed." Relying on such texts, Jesus outraged other Jews whose vision for what God's kingdom might look like differed radically from his own.

Jesus's actions and words clearly indicate that he believed that the "everlasting dominion" of God was arriving in and through what he did and said. Mark records Jesus's words at the beginning of his ministry, when he tells people to change their lives and orient them towards God, because "the time has come, the kingdom of God has arrived" (Mark 1:15). Jesus then embarks on what Mark portrays in his Gospel as a full-scale onslaught against the power of evil, delivering people from demons and healing those who were sick. Matthew's record of the Sermon on the Mount comes immediately after he recounts Jesus's kingdom-oriented activity in Galilee:

> Jesus went throughout Galilee, teaching in their synagogues, proclaiming the good news of the kingdom, and healing every disease and sickness among the people (Matt 4:23).

Having heard the announcement and seen the demonstration that the kingdom was arriving, we then get this lengthy block of Jesus's teaching known as the Sermon on the Mount, set at this point in Matthew's gospel to help his readers understand what the nature of this kingdom that Jesus has been proclaiming is, and how Jesus followers should live in the light of it.

And right in the middle of the Sermon, we get the Lord's Prayer, which now shows that although the kingdom, in one sense, is actually arriving, in another sense it is yet to come and Jesus followers need to pray for this—"let your kingdom come."

This is a tension that is followed right through the New Testament—often called "the now and the not yet" of the kingdom. We get it very clearly in the writings of Paul, who writes to Jesus followers in Rome to say that the kingdom of God is all about justice, peace, and joy in the Holy Spirit, clearly reflecting the present experience of these new, revolutionary Jesus communities. And he tells Colossian believers that God "has rescued us from the dominion of darkness and brought us into the kingdom of his beloved Son" (Col 1:13). At the same time, Paul looks forward to a time when "completeness" will come (1 Cor 13:10), when "creation itself will be liberated from its bondage to decay" (Rom 8:21), when God will reconcile all things to himself through the Messiah (Col 1:20), and to a day of resurrection when "we will be changed" (1 Cor 15:51).

So, although God's new day of world transformation had begun through Jesus, Jesus still taught his disciples to pray "your kingdom come." In another block of Jesus's teaching about the kingdom that Matthew has recorded for us, Jesus says that the kingdom of God is like the tiniest of mustard seeds, which, when planted, grows into an enormous flourishing tree (Matt 13:31–32). Although the New Testament writers looked forward to a future day of decisive fulfillment of the establishment of God's kingdom on earth, it's clear that they had an expectation that the world could be different even here and now. This vision of God coming to reclaim and transform his world—the kingdom of God—formed both the central core of Jesus's life and mission, and the life of the earliest Christians. Their sense was that God had done something decisive in the world, which he had called them to share; it was nothing less than a new way of being human that had repercussions for individuals, communities of Jesus followers, and as a result of that, the whole world. They understood that it was God's intention that "his wise, creative, loving presence and power [should] be reflected, 'imaged' if you like, into his world through his human creatures."[1] These communities understood Paul's assertion that the kingdom of God was justice, shalom, and joy in the Holy Spirit—and for the first three centuries we can trace the persistence of a Christian model of radical social concern that included support for widows, orphans, the elderly, and the sick, as well as countercultural attitudes towards groups that had low or no status in society, like women and slaves.

These tiny communities of Jesus followers that sprang up throughout the Roman world from the early decades of the first century onwards proclaimed that God's reign was being exercised *at that time* by one whom they acclaimed as the Lord, Jesus the Messiah, and had a real sense that their own communities were where this peaceful and joyous reign was being experienced, and that this reign was "destined to transform . . . history." This risen and living Lord, they believed, was exercising "his sovereignty over his people by banishing poverty and oppression and engendering new social relationships."[2]

1. Wright, *Surprised by Hope*, 218.

2. Gonzalez, *God's Reign and the End of Empires*, 212–13.

What emerges through all of this—the arrival of God's new day of blessing through Jesus, the sense of the great tree of transformation growing in the world and the eventual triumph of God's purposes—is a great sense of hope. Hope is absolutely central to Christian faith—hope for our own lives, hope for the world, hope for change in the here and now, hope for the ultimate triumph of justice, peace, and love. Tom Wright says, "'God's kingdom' in the preaching of Jesus refers, not to post-mortem destiny, not to our escape from this world into another one, but [to] God's sovereign rule coming 'on earth as it is in heaven.'"[3]

Wright goes on to say:

> To hope for a better future in this world—for the poor, the sick, the lonely and depressed, for the slaves, the refugees, the hungry and homeless, for the abused, the paranoid, the downtrodden and despairing, and in fact for the whole wide, wonderful and wounded world—is not something else, something extra, something tacked on to "the gospel" as an afterthought.[4]

Such a hope indeed is not an afterthought—it is absolutely integral to the gospel—the good news that God has come to reclaim and transform his world.

Hope in the Spirituals

Blues music has always managed to strike a note of hope in the midst of suffering. Part of this is because the blues has its roots in the black spirituals. These were songs that had their beginnings in the humiliation, the exploitation, and the suffering that was black slavery in the United States. We have a record of some 6,000 of these spirituals or "sorrow songs."

Slavery in America began in the seventeenth century. From the 1700s on, America was the land of opportunity and freedom for white Europeans; for black people, it meant one thing—bondage and dehumanization. Slavery meant being taken from your home and sailing to an unknown land in a fetid ship; being regarded as property; working fifteen to twenty hours a day, and being beaten for showing fatigue; being driven into the fields three days after giving birth; being sexually and physically abused as a matter of course.

3. Wright, *Surprised by Hope*, 25.
4. Ibid., 204.

Although the odds were stacked against them, black slaves were not quiescent—they resisted the bondage they suffered in a whole range of ways. One of these was the sort of religion they developed. The Christian faith embraced by many blacks in slavery was not just that of their masters. They eagerly asserted an idea of Christianity where freedom and liberation were to the fore and where black humanity was affirmed, despite everything that slavery and white people said.

So black people shouted and prayed, preached and sang about a God who was not confined to the powerful and the free. A God who was for them and loved them and who was their source of strength and dignity in the midst of the trials and hardships of life. A God to whom they looked for deliverance, not just when this life was over, but right now, from the torment of slavery.

For black slaves, the story of the deliverance of the children of Israel from Egypt was a formative one. Bruce Springsteen, with his *Seeger Sessions* band, recently brought one of these songs to a wider audience:

> O Mary don't you weep no more
> O Mary don't you weep no more
> Pharaoh's army got drownded
> O Mary don't you weep.

It's not hard to understand why this biblical event, so formative in Israel's history, should have become so important to black slaves. The exodus event speaks of a God who works within history to bring change and deliverance. So if God could do that for Hebrew slaves in Egypt, why could he not do it for black slaves in America?

In the spirituals, along with the deliverance from Egypt, other Old Testament stories keep appearing: Joshua and the battle of Jericho; Daniel in the lion's den; Daniel and his Hebrew friends in the fiery furnace. All of these are stories of God getting involved in the world and coming to the aid of his people. Black faith was grounded in the sense that God's liberation is at work in the world. God's righteousness or justice for them was not some religious concept—it was an affirmation of the power of God released in history for deliverance. One thing that becomes clear as we read about the God of the Bible is this: God is not a god who is distant and unknowable—rather, God is the God of history, who works and intervenes in our world to bring change and transformation.

James Cone comments, "Black slaves . . . knew that slavery contradicted humanity and divinity, and that was why they cited biblical references that focused on the liberation of the oppressed. . . . God is the liberator, the deliverer of the weak from the injustice of the strong."[5]

In the spirituals we find the aspirations for crossing over Jordan, reaching the promised land, and meeting those who have gone before. At first sight, these would appear to be simply a longing for a home in heaven after death, faith that there could be freedom and rest beyond the grave. This, of course, is part of the picture of Christian hope, comfort that has fortified many in the face of grave personal circumstances in life over the centuries. But there does seem to be more expressed in the songs sung by these slaves than simply the hope for going to heaven when you die. Here are the words of one ex-slave preacher:

> When I started preaching I couldn't read or write and had to preach what Master told me, and he says to tell them niggers iffen they obeys the master they goes to heaven; but I knowed there's something better for them, but daren't tell them 'cept on the sly. That I done lots. I tells 'em iffen they keeps praying, the Lord will set 'em free.[6]

Slaves clearly had to be very careful about how explicitly things were expressed, but it is likely that many of the references to freedom in the spirituals had at least a dual meaning. Heaven was not just some opiate for the slaves to make them more docile and submissive. While slaves with Christian faith looked forward to a heaven that existed beyond death, time, and space, they also longed for here-and-now, earthly places where freedom lay, like Canada, the northern US, and Africa. Talk of "glory" and "heaven," for many slaves, according to Cone, was not simply a spiritual freedom—it was "an eschatological freedom grounded in the events of the historical present, affirming that even now God's future is inconsistent with the realities of slavery."[7]

Harriet Tubman was a slave, who as a girl was badly beaten by various masters, leaving her suffering throughout her life from seizures, narcolepsy, and headaches. In 1849, she escaped to Canada and used a coded song, a kind of spiritual, to let her relatives and friends know that she intended to escape to freedom:

---

5. Cone, *The Spirituals and the Blues*, 28.

6. Botkin, *Lay My Burden Down*, 26.

7. Cone, *The Spirituals and the Blues*, 42.

When that there ole chariot comes
I'm goin' to leave you
I'm boun' for the promised land
Friends I'm goin' to leave you.

I'm sorry friends to leave you
Farewell! Farewell!
But I'll meet you in the mornin'
Farewell! Farewell!

I'll meet you in the mornin'
When you reach the promised land
On the other side of Jordan
For I'm boun' for the promised land.

When she reached freedom, she said, "I looked at my hands to see if I was the same person now I was free. There was such a glory over everything, the sun came like gold through the trees and over the fields, and I felt like I was in heaven." For eleven years, at great personal risk, Tubman returned repeatedly to the South, bringing, as she put it, "over 300 pieces of living and breathing property to the promised land." Later in life she would proudly say of her daring accomplishments, "I was conductor of the Underground Railroad for eight years, and I can say what most conductors can't say—I never ran my train off the track and I never lost a passenger."[8]

When helping slaves to escape, Tubman used spirituals as signals to hiding slaves to indicate whether it was safe to come out of hiding and continue on the journey. One song might be used as a warning song to stay hidden, and another to communicate that it was safe to come out of hiding. Tubman's favorite song, "Swing Low, Sweet Chariot" was used by slaves looking over the Ohio river—"I looked over Jordan and what did I see?" The chariot was the means of transport northward. The song "Steal Away" was used to alert fellow slaves to slip away for a secret slave meeting. "Wade in the Water" would caution slaves to travel along the riverbank so the dogs giving chase would be thrown off their scent. The use of devices such as these meant that there was no incriminating evidence for plantation owners or overseers to find.

Tubman had a strong Christian faith, trusted that God would keep her safe in her dangerous missions, and spoke of "consulting with God." Her belief in equality for everyone, which was expressed not just in her

---

8. Clinton, *Harriet Tubman*, 192.

antislavery efforts but in her support for women's suffrage, was fueled by her faith. She was sure that the New Testament texts that were used to support slavery were to be rejected, and she felt much more comfortable with the Old Testament stories of God's deliverance of his people. Tubman's faith clearly was not limited to a hope for heaven in the by and by, but was much more concretely rooted in the here and now, where she was sure God was still at work to bring liberation.

And yes, of course there was the sense as well of heaven being a transcendent future where the oppressed would "lay down that heavy load" in "that great gettin' up morning."

In that day, there would be:

> No more hard trial in the kingdom;
> no more tribulation, no more parting,
> no more quarreling, backbiting in the kingdom
> No more sunshine for to bu'n you,
> no more rain for to wet you
> Every day will be Sunday in heaven.[9]

Hope beyond the grave, of course, has always been a vital part of Christian faith. Right at the outset, in the Roman world of the first century AD, Christians, like most of the population of the urban centers, were poor—they were not part of the small numbers of the elite in this world. Like the poor everywhere, their lives were uncertain and hard, and death was an ever-present reality—infant mortality was high and life expectancy low. Many Christians were slaves, beaten and abused as a matter of course. On top of that was the ill will of their pagan neighbors, who suspected these members of this new Jewish sect of displeasing the gods and bringing misfortune to their neighborhood. In such situations, hope for new life, resurrection life after death, would have added a new dimension to the lives of these Jesus followers. It was, no doubt, partly the reason for Christianity's rapid spread throughout the empire and the reason so many Christians showed such courage in the face of persecution and the threat of execution at various periods during the early centuries.

But the hope offered by Christian faith was not just for the future—it was also a hope for the present, as Christian communities lived a new communal life under the lordship of Jesus the Messiah, loving, supporting, and caring for one another in the midst of a harsh and unforgiving environment. These Jesus communities were the source of hope that the world

9. Cone, *The Spirituals and the Blues*, 89.

could be different. Harriet Tubman and other black slaves reflect the same type of faith and hope—hope, yes, for something better after death, but hope, also, that things could change, that deliverance and freedom could come. The God of the Bible, the God of history was their God too, and surely he would bring deliverance.

Hope in the Blues

"The blues and the spirituals flow from the same bedrock of experience, and neither is an adequate interpretation of black life without the commentary of the other."[10] The troubles that underpin the spirituals are there in the blues too. A well-worn phrase in the blues is the "worried blues"—both spirituals and the blues expressed the deep worry of blacks about their lives. We have already noted Leadbelly's comment that it was black slavery that gave rise to the blues and that it was the result of worried minds. The blues gave expression to real and deep-seated anxieties about life—but, as well, it gave some ease to the worried mind.

Mississippi bluesman Willie King, talking about the early Delta blues, said, "The good Lord in his spirit had to send somethin' down to the people to help ease they worried mind. And that where the music come in—it would work in what you tryin' a do, what you strivin' for, to help give you a vision of a brighter day way up ahead, to help you get your mind offa what you are in right now . . . and the blues, like John Lee Hooker says, 'is a healer.'"[11] The blues is partly about suffering and partly about hope.

Singing about the hard times, yes, but looking for a better day ahead as well. "There must be a better world somewhere," sings B. B. King, putting it quite forthrightly. In many blues songs there is an aspiration for a better place, a better time up ahead. "Trouble in Mind" is an old blues song recorded by Big Bill Broonzy, Sister Rosetta Tharpe, Snooks Eaglin, and Johnny Shines amongst many others. In it the singer is in such a bad place that he wants to find "some old railyard iron" to lay his head on and to let "that 2.19 Special pacify my mind." Suicide is on the agenda here, and yet, the refrain of the song still somehow, in the midst of the darkness, is hoping for something better:

---

10. Ibid., 100.

11. From an interview in Scorsese, director, *Feel Like Going Home.*

> Trouble in mind, well I'm blue
> But I won't be blue always
> Sun's gonna shine in my backyard some day.

Somewhere in the reality of oppression, trouble, and a feeling of helplessness, the despair gives way to hope. Terry and McGhee's "Better Day" complains that "I don't have a dime" and "I need a break," but goes on to say,

> That's alright
> I don't worry anymore
> There will be a better day.

The aspiration is all the more remarkable when you realize that Brownie McGhee, the guitar player in the duo, had been crippled by polio in his legs, and Terry, the harmonica player, had been blinded in both eyes through a series of accidents.

One of the most recorded blues songs of all time is "Worried Life Blues," originally recorded by Major "Big Maceo" Merriweather in 1941, but then by literally hundreds of artists, including B. B. King on his 2000 album with Eric Clapton, *Riding with the King*. The song, very typically, is about a lost love: "Oh lordy lord, oh lordy lord, It hurts me so bad, for us to part . . . I've been worried, grieving my life alone." But the last line of each despairing verse says, "But someday baby, I ain't gonna worry my life anymore." Somehow the singer knows that the pain is going to pass and things are going to get better.

We might also note the frequency with which trains, highways, and buses occur in the blues. Aside from the "ramblin'" nature of the itinerant bluesman, there's a sense of wanting to move on, move forward to something that is better in another place, at another time.

On the subject of hope in the blues, James Cone says, "It is true that hopelessness is an authentic aspect of the blues' experience, and despair is a central theme in the blues. . . . [But] the blues express a belief that one day things will not be like what they are today."[12]

It is the case, as well, that many of the spirituals were carried over into the blues repertoire and they certainly carry this suffering-hope duality. There are songs like "Woke up this Mornin' with My Mind Stayed on Jesus" and "I Want Jesus to Walk with Me," both expressing the comforting presence of Jesus in the midst of troubles, or "Wade in the Water," which refers to God bringing healing after the angel of John 5:4 "troubles the water."

12. Ibid., 123.

As well as the presence of the spirituals in the blues, though, we have a long history of what we might call "gospel blues," songs performed in the blues idiom by blues artists with Christian faith. For some artists, their Christian faith gave a sense of a God who walked with them in their troubles and to whom they looked for deliverance. There is a rich seam of this sort of music, running from the early Delta blues right through to the present.

Blind Willie Johnson is the most obvious early example of this. When Willie was seven, he was blinded by an incident in his home. Johnson remained poor throughout his life, preaching and singing for tips in the streets of a number of Texas cities. In 1945, he began to live in the ruins of his home which had burned to the ground and ended up contracting malarial fever and dying shortly after. Willie's was a hard life, even by the standards of the early blues artists, but he composed and recorded many gospel blues songs that have stood the test of time and are regularly performed today. Songs like "Keep Your Lamps Trimmed and Burning," "Praise God I'm Satisfied," "The Soul of a Man," "Nobody's Fault But Mine," "John the Revelator" and "God Don't Never Change" have been covered by artists as diverse as The Rolling Stones, Tom Jones, Bruce Cockburn, and the Grateful Dead.

Willie's gospel songs are suffused with hope—take "God Don't Never Change," for example. The song, sounding raw in Willie's rasping voice, is essentially a meditation on Psalm 139, where the question addressed to God is, "Where could I go to escape your presence?" God's the creator, God's up in heaven, God's down in hell, he's in the pulpit, he's all over the floor, sings Willie. But most significantly, God is right with Willie in the difficulties of life—"God in the time of sickness . . . In the time of the influenza, He truly was a God to you." In the midst of the sorrows of his life, Willie wrote "Praise God I'm Satisfied," quite remarkably singing of "joy and gladness," and knowing that "I'm a child of his." That was the source of deep satisfaction for this blind musician.

God's way of fixing the world is through the life, death, and resurrection of Jesus, which brings both personal hope and hope for the whole world. The gospel blues hits the note of personal redemption and hope loud and clear. Blind Willie Johnson sang "I Know His Blood Can Make Me Whole" in 1927 and "Let Your Light Shine on Me" in 1929. If we fast-forward a few decades we have Rev. Gary Davis, an outstanding acoustic guitar player and blues artist, singing, "there's been a great change since I been born," referring of course to new birth in Christ. He sings "things that I used to do, I don't do no more." Ray Charles hits the same note of repentance in his song "Sinners Prayer"—"Well if I've been a bad boy baby I declare I'll change my ways" followed by "Please have mercy Lord have mercy on me; Well if I've done somebody wrong Lord have mercy if you please."

Bang up to date, Kelly Joe Phelps, on his stunning album of gospel blues in 2012, *Brother Sinner and the Whale*, gives us a very intimate and personal insight into the power of the gospel for personal transformation. In the song "Goodbye to Sorrow," the child that was lost, without a home is now "redeemed" and "washed clean." In "Pilgrim's Reach," Phelps talks of going "the wrong way again, walking away from Calvary and right back into sin. And then in "I've Been Converted" he sings, "When I was a sinner . . . a voice came from heaven, saying, 'I will show you the way.'" The result is "I know I've been converted," with the added challenge, "do you?"

As we have seen, Christian hope is ultimately centered around the idea of bodily resurrection whereby God's children can share in God's new transformed world. This is reflected in "Ain't No Grave Can Hold My Body Down," originally written by "Brother" Claude Ely, a songwriter and Pentecostal holiness preacher, with a raw, bluesy version recorded by Bozie Sturdivant in 1942, and then famously recorded by Johnny Cash a few months before his death in 2003.

> There ain't no grave can hold my body down.
> When I hear that trumpet sound
> I'm gonna rise right outta the ground
> Ain't no grave that can hold my body down.
>
> Well look way down the river and what do you think I see?
> I see a band of angels and they're coming after me.
> There ain't no grave that can hold my body down.

Cash's voice is that of an old man, and yet is clear and convincing over the sparse instrumentation. The recording is both sobering and powerful. Rick Rubin, who produced the album, recollects a conversation in May 2003 with Johnny Cash soon after his wife June had died:

> I'd never heard him so distraught. And he said, 'You know, I've been through tremendous pain in my life, and I've never felt anything like this.' . . .
> . . . He sounded so weak, so beaten, and I'd never really heard him like that before. I'm not sure where the question came from, but I said, 'Do you feel like somewhere you can find faith?' And

when he heard that word, a switch went off in his head, and he answered in a strong voice, 'My faith is UNSHAKABLE.' And the conversation changed after that. So he had tremendous faith, he didn't really have fear and he already was dealing with pain; I think he had acceptance. When he knew he was going to die, he was calm and matter of fact about it, and . . . that was it.[13]

An integral part of Cash's Christian faith was the hope of resurrection. This has been the case since the very earliest days of Christianity. Within twenty years or so of the first Easter, Paul the apostle told the Jesus followers in Corinth—"if the Messiah has not been resurrected, then your faith is useless" (1 Cor 15:17). Paul didn't think there was much point in following someone who had simply brought a new philosophy to the world—such people were ten a penny in Paul's day—one more dead philosopher or would-be Messiah was neither here nor there. The point was, though, Paul, along with a load of people he actually knew, had seen the risen Jesus—and he goes on to explain that the Messiah's resurrection was the "firstfruits"— the first and the guarantee—for believers who "fall asleep," in other words, who die (1 Cor 15:20). The Messiah's death and resurrection brought a "new creation" (2 Cor 5:17) which Christians could share in—the new life of the Messiah infusing Jesus followers right now, and then raising them to life at the last. This is the Christian hope, this was the essence of Cash's faith, this is what Ely's song expresses.

We get this same hope reflected in "Ain't No Grave Can Hold His Body Down" by the North Mississippi Allstars, composed by Luther Dickinson on the death of his father. Dickinson talks about having to "face the one thing we all have to do," and hopes to be "as brave as he was on judgment day." The song talks about "having no fear," because "no grave can hold his body down." On this same theme, Mississippi Fred McDowell's "You Gotta Move," covered by many people, including The Rolling Stones, is also a song about resurrection—"when the Lord gets ready, you gotta move." One gets the sense in the song of Ezekiel's dry bones moving together at the sound of the Lord's voice—when God's good and ready, them bones gotta move! Christian hope is not about some disembodied spiritual existence—it revolves around physical resurrection to share in God's new, remade world.

As we have seen, there is a lot more to the gospel than God simply sorting out individuals—important though that is. The Bible's story is of a God who wants to fix his broken world and sort out the problem of evil;

13. Kornbluth, "Johnny Cash's 'Ain't No Grave,'" *Huffington Post*, November 9, 2010.

and that through the life, death, and resurrection of Jesus God has done that—in such a way that Jesus followers can experience the new world, the new creation God is making right now and can begin to demonstrate that to a needy world. Jesus followers also look forward to a day when God will complete his world transformation project and bring in the fullness of his justice, peace, and love. This is the biblical idea of heaven—not some golden city in the sky, but a world changed and transformed. This is celebrated in an old traditional blues song, "Satan Your Kingdom Must Come Down," recorded recently by Robert Plant and the Band of Joy. The song is based on Luke 10:18, and rejoices with Jesus in the fall of Satan:

> Gonna shout till they tear your kingdom down
> I heard the voice of Jesus say
> Satan, your kingdom must come down.

The ultimate goal of the gospel story is the end of evil and a coming new world of love and justice, which will be shared by believers in new resurrection bodies.

But part of all this is the responsibility of Jesus followers to anticipate God's new day and to pursue right now the peace and justice that are the characteristics of the world to which Christian hope points. In his 2012 album, *Blues for the Modern Daze,* in a song entitled "Brother's Keeper," Walter Trout sings, "Jesus says to feed the hungry, Jesus said to help the poor, Some of those so-called Christians, they don't believe in that no more." Walter's just echoing the New Testament—if you see a brother or sister in need and you refuse to help, how can you say the love of God lives in you (1 John 3:17)?

Tom Wright argues strongly for the need for Jesus followers to bring the hope of the future into the present. "We must . . . claim [the world] for the kingdom of God, for the lordship of Jesus, and in the power of the Spirit, so that we can then go out and work for that kingdom, announce that lordship, and effect change through that power." He goes on to say that because Jesus is risen and has been installed as Lord of the whole world,

> The world has already been turned upside down; that's what Easter is all about. It isn't a matter of waiting until God eventually does something different at the end of time. God has brought his future, his putting-the-world-to-rights future, into the present in Jesus of Nazareth, and he wants that future to be implicated more and more in the present. That's what we pray for every time we say

the Lord's Prayer: Thy kingdom come, thy will be done, on earth as it is in heaven.[14]

The blues is a potent reminder of the possibility of hope in the midst of struggle. The story of the Bible, too, is really the story of hope in the midst of trial and struggle. We see it time and time again in the individual stories. But we see it most of all in the big story, where the hope of the Old Testament prophets is for a brand new day of peace, joy, and freedom that God would bring in; where Jesus proclaimed that this new day was arriving in and through himself; and where the New Testament writers joyfully proclaim that indeed that day had arrived with the death and resurrection of the Messiah. Again, the hope here is not for some nebulous golden city in the sky, but for a brand new world that God would make, and even now is beginning to create through Christ. Hope breaks into the suffering and anguish of the world through the glimpses of God's new world that his people are able to show. Insofar as we participate in God's world-transformation project, we create hope and new possibilities in the midst of darkness that one day will give way to God's brand new day.

Recommended Listening

Eric Bibb, *Twelve Gates to The City,* Luna Records, 2006

Bruce Springsteen, *We Shall Overcome: The Seeger Sessions*, SonyBMG, 2006

B. B. King, *His Definitive Greatest Hits,* Universal, 1999

Kelly Joe Phelps, *Brother Sinner and the Whale,* Continental Song City, 2012

North Mississippi Allstars, *Keys To The Kingdom,* BMI, 2011

14. Wright, *Surprised by Hope,* 276, 226.

six

Shaking Off the Modern Daze

Do not store up for yourselves treasures on earth, where moth and rust consume and where thieves break in and steal; but store up for yourselves treasures in heaven, where neither moth nor rust consumes and where thieves do not break in and steal. For where your treasure is, there your heart will be also. The eye is the lamp of the body. So, if your eye is healthy, your whole body will be full of light; but if your eye is unhealthy, your whole body will be full of darkness. If then the light in you is darkness, how great is the darkness! No one can serve two masters; for a slave will either hate the one and love the other, or be devoted to the one and despise the other. You cannot serve God and wealth. Therefore I tell you, do not worry about your life, what you will eat or what you will drink, or about your body, what you will wear. Is not life more than food, and the body more than clothing?

MATTHEW 6:19–25

Nobody Knows You When You're Down and Out

As we have seen, the context for the emergence of the blues was a situation of oppression and suffering for African Americans in the Southern states. Segregation, disenfranchisement, lynch violence and shocking poverty all created an environment where expressions of "worry," "troubled minds," and the "worst old feeling I ever had" in blues songs were entirely natural and understandable. W. E. B. Du Bois, traveling through

Georgia thirty-five years after slavery ended said he had found "the Negro problem in its naked dirt and penury."[1] The cotton sharecropping system largely left black workers deep in debt. Du Bois records many stories of blacks being cheated of their earnings or turned off their lands. One black farmer told him that he had worked for forty-five years, "beginning with nothing and still having nothing."[2]

Litwack sums up the black experience at this time by observing that neither "renting nor hard work and frugality could overcome the hopeless cycle of work, debt, and poverty that so sharply circumscribed the economic freedom of black Southerners."[3] All the indices for health, access to healthcare, education, and social conditions for blacks under Jim Crow were at appallingly low levels, with disease and preventable death being commonplace.[4] Poverty largely defined the way of life during this period for Southern blacks. John Perkins, who grew up in Mississippi in the 1930s, says of the Deep South during the Depression, "Economic hardship and despair pretty much dominated all of life in the black community."[5]

The blues attests to this poverty, with songs about lack of money, lack of employment, and ill health being commonplace. Consider Big Bill Broonzy's "Starvation Blues" from 1934, where he sings about having no job, no place to stay, being "mistreated 'cause I'm down," and that "starvation [is] here, starvation everywhere I go":

> Starvation in my kitchen, rent sign's on my do',
> If my luck don't change, can't see that Mama home no mo'.
> . . . When I had my money, my doorbell rung every day
> So now I ain't got no money, my friends goin' the other way.

Big Joe Williams's 1937 song "I Won't Be in Hard Luck No More" expresses the same sentiment:

> I had money baby, I even had friends for miles around
> Well all the money gone: oh well and my friends cannot be
> found.

---

1. Du Bois, *The Souls of Black Folks,* 57.

2. Ibid., 61.

3. Litwack, *Trouble in Mind,* 137.

4. See ibid. Chapters 2 and 7 give details of both education and the effects of poverty under Jim Crow.

5. Perkins, *Let Justice Roll Down,* 28.

As does Jimmy Cox's "Nobody Knows You When You're Down and Out," written in 1923 and first recorded and made popular by Bessie Smith in 1929. The song talks about "not a penny in your pocket," falling "so low," losing all your friends, and having "nowhere to go."

The blues have continued to document the experiences of poverty by black communities through the decades. In the 1950s, J. B. Lenoir recorded "Eisenhower Blues"—"Ain't got a dime, ain't even got a cent, I don't even have no money, to pay my rent," and in 1961, Johnny Guitar Watson sings in "Broke and Lonely" that "I'm broke and I'm lonely and my heart's in misery."

More up-to-date, Albert Collins recorded "When the Welfare Turns Its Back on You" in 1977. It contains the sobering line, "Now you look all through your house, Yes, you can't find a piece of bread." And in 2009, Robert Cray recorded "Night Patrol," which deals frankly with the subject of homelessness:

> See him huddled in the shadows, sleepin' on his cardboard bed.
> Usin' rags for a pillow, where he lays his unwashed head.
> His blankets old newspapers, they're not much good against the snow.
> You see so many out there like him, when you walk the night patrol,
> When you walk the night patrol.

Mississippi John Hurt, who first recorded in the 1920s, and was rediscovered in the 1960s, sums up the experience of poverty in his 1966 recording of "Trouble I Had It All My Days":

> Well trouble, trouble, I had it all my days.
> Trouble, had it all my days.
> Seem like trouble, gonna carry me to my grave.

You Cannot Serve God and Wealth

Jesus's teachings in the Sermon on the Mount make uncomfortable reading for Christians in the wealthy regions of the world such as the US and Europe. He says quite bluntly—"Stop collecting treasures for your own benefit on earth," and "You cannot serve God and wealth."

The problem for us is that our whole way of life is predicated on collecting treasure for our own benefit and on serving wealth. Economic growth is the driver for the modern nation-states in which we live and work. For economies to grow, they need to produce more, and produce it more efficiently. Consequently there needs to be a level of consumption commensurate with the production. Growth and consumption are two sides of the same coin. The inevitable result is, on the one hand, an unending drive for more efficient production, lower costs, and ever more labor force productivity, and on the other limitless consumption of goods, many of which we do not actually need. We thus are bombarded with relentless sales, marketing, and advertising messages to ensure the whole system continues to function.

Walter Brueggemann describes our modern way of life as the "global market economy supported by an undisciplined militarism in the service of a limitless consumer entitlement." Examining the system of oppression under which the ancient Hebrew slaves lived under Pharaoh, he characterizes it as one of "anxious production and predatory covetousness." The parallels with our modern age are obvious. Brueggemann says, however, that "the pharaonic enterprise among us is not legitimate and need not be the story of our life."[6] Using scripture as a guide, Antonio Gonzalez, too, has analyzed the state of the world and finds that our modern globalized economy shares with all other empires and regimes the theme of domination, which necessitates inequality, extremes of wealth and poverty, expansionism, ecological devastation, and violence for maintaining itself.[7]

In the 2010 movie *Wall Street: Money Never Sleeps*, there is a scene in which the young whiz kid banker, Jake Moore, asks the unscrupulous head of Churchill Swartz Investment Bank, Bretton James, "What's your number?" James looks back, a little puzzled, "My number?" "Yes," Moore explains, "everybody's got a number, the price at which they can be bought. What's yours?" James thinks for a moment and simply says, "More." That moment sums up the character of Bretton James and, indeed, the spirit of the banking environment over recent years. But perhaps, when we think about it, for many of us it also sums up ourselves, as well. The whole story of our society, our economy, sweeps us along on a great tide called "more."

Our consuming, acquisitive way of life, however, in which many of us share, is deeply problematic when we come face-to-face with Jesus's teaching. And in case we think that these words of Jesus are in some sense secondary matters, we need to understand that Jesus spoke a great deal about money and the way in which his followers were to handle possessions. This

---

6. Brueggemann, *Disruptive Grace*, 88, 89.

7. Gonzalez, *God's Reign and the End of Empires*, 77–79.

was probably the most prominent theme within his overall teaching about the kingdom of God.

Jesus called for a radical commitment to the now-arriving kingdom of God, which required utter commitment (see the sayings about the kingdom at Matthew 13:44ff.), even beyond that to family (Luke 9:57ff.). Such a commitment required a complete trust in the goodness and provision of God, so that the more mundane matters of life, such as food and clothing, could be left in God's hands. For Jesus, this radical commitment would go so much against the grain of the world around that it was likely it would bring persecution and suffering (Matt 5:10–12; Matt 10:17–19). The implication for lifestyle, then, is that it must be "viewed from the perspective of the kingdom."[8] For Jesus, a commitment to the kingdom and the attendant utter trust in God meant his followers needed to keep themselves detached from anything that would distract them from the kingdom commitment.

And the number one thing that could possibly distract his followers, according to Jesus, was money and possessions. We need only think of Jesus's advice to the rich young ruler to "go sell everything you have and distribute the money to the poor" (Luke 18:22), the parable of the rich farmer who built ever bigger barns for storing his produce and is condemned for "hoarding things for himself instead of becoming rich in the sight of God" (Luke 12:21), or Jesus's statement, which his disciples found so astonishing, that it's "easier for a camel to squeeze through the eye of a needle than for a rich person to enter God's kingdom" (Matt 19:24).

We often squirm off the hook here by saying that it's one's *attitude* to money that Jesus is most concerned about, but in the light of what he actually says, we cannot escape so easily. Actually having riches, according to Jesus, represens a huge obstacle to living in God's new kingdom. For Jesus, the arrival of God's kingdom meant that there was a new way of being human, and that entailed a fundamental reorientation which was founded on utter trust on God. "Why do you worry?" he asked his followers in Matthew 6. "Don't worry about food or drink or clothing, because your heavenly father knows you need these things. God will provide what you need—you concentrate on desiring earnestly God's kingdom and his justice."

This represents a huge challenge to people living in a society where every advertisement we see, every magazine we read, every TV program we watch, urges us to consume more and more. Technology continues to develop at an incredible pace, creating ever-new opportunities for commerce,

8. Davids, "New Testament Foundations for Living More Simply," 42.

entertainment, and access to information on anything and everything. We need to keep up, to upgrade, to engage, be part of the conversation—or else we'll be hopelessly left behind, technophobic dinosaurs, unbeautified, uncool, unloved.

Into the spiralling consumption of modern life, Jesus's words ring uncomfortably in our ears, "You cannot serve God and wealth." There doesn't seem to be much of a get-out clause here for Jesus followers. It's either-or, it's one or the other.

Good News to the Poor

It's hard for those of us who live in the small part of the world that is economically comfortable to imagine that, actually, we are in the minority, and that a great proportion of the world does not live in the way that we take for granted. The reality, as we have seen, is that over 3 billion people live on less than $2.50 a day and 1.4 billion on half that amount. The stark fact is that nearly half of the people on our planet live in grinding, dehumanizing poverty. And inequality between the rich and the poor is greater than it's ever been. One billion people living in the world's wealthiest countries account for over three-quarters of the world's GDP, while nearly half the world's population, who live in the poorest countries, account for only 3.3 percent.[9]

The wealth that most people reading this enjoy is unprecedented in the history of the world—what we take for the norm is, actually, unusual both historically and geographically. Take the people who first heard Jesus preach in Galilee or the first groups of Jesus followers in the tiny Christian communities in the urban centers of the Mediterranean world of the first century. We can tell by the stories that Jesus told that his audience was made up of working people, peasants, day laborers, people who knew what sort of personal disaster it was to lose a coin and need to search high and low for it, who knew widows in their communities who could hardly afford to give away a "mite"—about half the value of the lowest denomination Roman coin in circulation—and who were anxious about where their next meal was coming from.

And what we know about the Roman Empire is that there were a small number of people at the top of society, but that there were in excess of 95

9. According to the World Bank. See the "Data on Poverty and Inequality" section at http:web.worldbank.org

percent of people living in what we would consider to be poverty.[10] This composition was likely mirrored in the Christian communities, with most early Jesus followers living in conditions that today we would associate with developing world slum communities, with all the attendant difficulties of that life, ranging from malnourishment to lack of clean drinking water to poor sanitation to waterborne diseases—all resulting in ill health, low life expectancy, and high infant mortality. A recent study by English scholar Peter Oakes analyzed the likely composition of one of the Christian groups in Rome at the time Paul wrote to them and concluded that they likely included slaves, homeless people, migrant workers, and some craft workers.[11] These were people who were just about getting by and for whom daily life was difficult and destitution not that far away.

When Paul asked the Roman Christians in chapter 8 of his letter what it was that might separate them from Christ's love—trouble, or distress, or harassment, or famine, or nakedness, or danger, or sword—he was not using hyperbole to make a point. Rather, these were all real perils of life in the capital of the empire for the Jesus followers to whom Paul wrote. Trouble was near at hand—the death of a child, a fire that might sweep through your neighborhood, difficulty in making enough money to feed yourself and your family, or harassment from those around who were suspicious of people who didn't honor the gods.

So it has always been for the poor. As (relatively) wealthy Americans or Europeans, our lives, for the most part, are characterized by choice—whether it's what we eat or drink or wear or how we choose to be entertained. Half of the people in our world simply do not have these choices; their lives are defined by lack and the need to survive. They would relate readily to Paul's list of dangers in Romans 8. The realization that, beyond all the difficulty and harshness that life throws at you, there is God's love, a love which, moreover, is made real and actualized by a living, breathing family of loving brothers and sisters of faith, truly brings a sense of victory—"in all these things we are super-conquerors through him who loved us," Paul concludes.

To these first Christians, the gospel was truly liberating good news. Through it they discovered that they were not, after all, nobodies, the refuse

---

10. Recent studies by Meggitt, *Paul, Poverty and Survival,* and Longenecker, *Remember the Poor,* carefully analyze poverty in the first century and agree that poverty was endemic and a middle class such as we know it was absent from that world.

11. Oakes, *Reading Romans in Pompeii.*

of society. One of the prized social values in Roman society was that of gaining glory. Glory, honor, and esteem were what the Roman nobleman sought through his position, wealth, status, rhetorical skill, or battle experience. Society was highly stratified and it was clear to rich and poor alike where the lines were drawn. The people at the bottom who were the members of the Christian house churches assuredly did not share in the glory of the empire. But Paul turns the table on the way of the world in his letter to the Romans, assuring the believers that it is they, rather than the Roman elite, who can expect glory and honor—"there will be glory and honor for all who do good" (Rom 2:10); "by faith . . . we boast in the hope of God's glory" (Rom 5:2); "the present suffering is nothing compared with the coming glory" (Rom 8:18).[12]

One of the things that you notice when you spend time with the world's poor is the poor self-image that they have. As I have met with desperately poor people in urban slums or in rural villages throughout India, what I have seen is the way that people will often not even make eye contact with you. They are ashamed and feel unworthy in your presence. Poverty is not just physical, it's emotional and spiritual as well; it brings a poverty of spirit. The gospel, however, the good news that God has broken into the world to bring salvation and healing to everyone, to rich and poor alike, is especially good news to the poor. Because first and foremost it says to everyone, you are valued, you are special, God loves you. Archbishop Desmond Tutu says, "Can you imagine what the gospel means to people whose dignity is downtrodden underfoot every day of their lives, to those who have had their noses rubbed in the dust as if they didn't count?" He stresses that the essence of the gospel lies in God's love and God's desire for justice. The good news, he says, is "that God loved us, that God loves us, and that God will love us forever unchangingly."[13] To those with nothing, the gospel brings a whole new way of seeing the world.

Not only, however, does the gospel make a spiritual difference to people, it makes—or should make—a physical difference as well. This is because the gospel is not simply about individual spiritual salvation; rather, it is primarily about God creating a community through which God is beginning to renew and remake the world. We've already thought about this idea of the kingdom of God, of God breaking in through the life, death,

---

12. Jewett, *Romans,* discusses the cultural significance of Paul's various references to glory in his letter.

13. Tutu, *God Has a Dream,* 63, 35.

and resurrection of Jesus the Messiah to rule God's world again, bringing peace and shalom. Where this gets worked out and demonstrated in the first instance is through God's people, through groups of Jesus followers.

Thinking back to the first followers of Jesus, they discovered the reality of what Paul called a "new creation," a new way of being human together in their communities. This was the way of love, of mutual support, of help, service, and kindness. What new disciples found in these first communities was the dynamic presence of Jesus himself, which enabled Christians "to establish right now, within the basic structures of the old society, a new form of social organization."[14]

They discovered, as Paul says in 2 Corinthians 5:17, that there was indeed a new creation, that "everything old has passed away; see, everything has become new!" New neighborliness, new solidarity, new practices of justice and love were the order of the day in these Jesus communities.

It seems certain that the concern for the poor that we see so readily in the life of Jesus was a fundamental element in the life the early Christians. We know that the very first groups of Jesus followers "were united and shared everything in common" (Acts 2:44) and that they immediately set up means of caring for the most vulnerable amongst them (Acts 6). But as we read on through the New Testament, we find this same love and care built into the fabric of their communities.

John Knox has suggested that there is "plenty of evidence in Paul's letters that the churches were expected to care for the poor."[15] More recently Bruce Longenecker, in a comprehensive study of Paul's attitude to poverty, concludes that Paul was "uncompromising in promoting care for the poor as integral to the practice and theology engendered within Jesus-groups." Of major importance in this regard is the collection that Paul mentions on a number of occasions within his letters, that he was taking for the poor among Jerusalem Jesus followers (e.g., Romans 15:25ff.). A number of scholars recently have picked up on Paul's encouragement to believers in Galatia "not to grow weary in well-doing . . . as often as God gives the opportunity, let us work for the good of all people" (Gal 6:9–10). The phrase used here, "doing the good," appears to be "(virtually) technical terminology in the ancient world for bestowing material benefits on others."[16] Care

14. Gonzalez, *God's Reign and the End of Empires*, 220.

15. Knox, *Chapters in a Life of Paul*, 28.

16. Longenecker, *Remember the Poor*, 142. See also Winter, *Seek the Welfare of the City*, 11–40; and Wright, *Paul for Everyone*, 79.

for the needy, it seems, as we read through Paul's letters and take note of the many relevant references, was a mark of these first Christian communities.[17] In the Ephesian letter, the author indicates the kind of behavior that the new Christians undertake, including, in 4:18, "sharing with the needy"—evidence "for the continuance of communal sharing of possessions among the early Christians."[18]

Mutual love and support continued to be the hallmark of the Christian groups in the early centuries and it was noticed by those around them. Christian leader Tertullian, writing in the second century, noted that it was said of Christians, "See how they love one another . . . and how they are ready to die for one another." And on through to the fourth century, with the Roman emperor Julian, who considered Christians to be "impious," but who recognized the success of the Christian mission had been because of their caring for strangers and burying the dead. He wrote, "The impious Galileans did not content themselves with feeding their own poor, but gave food also to our people."[19]

It is also worth noting the way Aristides of Athens, who wrote in the second century, describes the alternative way of life of Christians, which was quite at odds with the world around them:

> They live in all humility and gentleness. . . . They love one another and do not despise widows: they free orphans from whoever would treat them with violence. Those who have give to those who have nothing. As soon as they see a foreigner, they take him into their own houses, and they rejoice with him as with a real brother. . . . If any among them . . . is poor or needy and they themselves do not have abundant means, they fast for two or three days to remedy the lack of livelihood among the needy.[20]

From the very beginnings, the Christian gospel was good news to the poor. It presented a new vision for the way the world should be, based on the reality of the inbreaking rule of God. The citizens of the Roman Empire who became Jesus followers entered communities that celebrated justice, fairness, love, and the peace of the God's kingdom. Mutual support and care

---

17. See e.g., Gal 2:10; 2 Cor 5:14; 1 Thess 5:14; Rom 12:13, 16; 2 Thess 3:13; 1 Tim 5:3ff.; Titus 3:14.

18. Best, *Ephesians*, 455.

19. Julian, *The Works of the Emperor Julian*, Ep.22.430D.

20. Aristides, *Apologia*, Syrian version, xv, 6–10, quoted in Gonzalez, *God's Reign and the End of Empires*, 209.

for others around them were fundamental to their faith. The gospel brought salvation in every sense of the word—it brought the shalom of God's kingdom, a wholeness that included the spiritual, the physical, and the social. To people whose lives were difficult and full of trouble, these communities were transformational. They brought people not only into faith, but into love and hope—and into a new way of life, a new way of being human. The gospel, from the beginning, was good news to the poor.

Attitude to Riches

It is important to note as well that material wealth, for the early Christians, was not to be envied or grasped at. As we have seen, Jesus said quite flatly, "you cannot serve God and money." It seems that the two were incompatible. For Jesus, God and money were two quite different lords, and serving money precluded you from serving God. In the same vein, Paul, reflecting the view of early Jesus followers, says that greed and the accumulation of money is "idolatry" (e.g., Col 3:5). Commenting on this, Gonzalez says, "Exaltation of wealth . . . is not simply an ethical fault; it is authentic separation from the living God."[21]

In a recent study on the subject of how greed is treated in the Bible, Brian Rosner shows that the way in which the idea of greed is equated with idolatry in the New Testament "is a powerful means of condemning greed, since idolatry was the most serious of sins." He goes on to say that the New Testament view was that, "To have a strong desire to acquire and keep for yourself more and more money and material things is an attack on God's exclusive rights to human love and devotion, trust and confidence, and service and obedience."[22]

The author of the first letter to Timothy considered the love of money to be "a root of all kinds of evil" (1 Tim 6:10) and said that an attachment to money had separated many from the faith. For us who live in modern, technological, growth-oriented economies, this seems hard to grasp. Accumulation is built in to the very fabric of our way of life, and who in his right mind doesn't want just a little more money? Our modern idea of faith as a privatized spirituality, as assent to a set of theological propositions, or to church attendance, or of being basically a decent person, leaves plenty of room for money. If faith equates to a one-on-one, internal relationship with

21. Gonzalez, *God's Reign and the End of Empires*, 228.

22. Rosner, *Greed as Idolatry*, 172–73.

God, along with a clean-looking middle-class life with church attendance thrown in, then there is no reason why having and wanting to acquire money should matter all that much. But if faith is discipleship in the kingdom of God, living a life that acknowledges there is a new way of being human that has broken into the world, that reaches forward into God's future to bring into the present a new world of justice and love, then suddenly our attitude to money comes center stage. Living under the reign of the Messiah changes everything—greed, acquisitiveness, consumerism all become false gods that must be renounced so that the vibrant life of the new humanity can flourish in our own lives and those whose lives we touch.

It is hard for us to even see our way past the way things are and our own complicity in it, to a sense that there could be another way to live. A way that goes not just beyond self-absorbed materialism to simply "giving back" a bit and showing some compassion to those less fortunate, but a way that chooses to serve God at the expense of personal promotion and gain, and demonstrates and seeks a more just way of living. That is the challenge that faces us, however. The gospel, which is such good news to the poor, which lifts their spirits and brings new hope and care through the community of faith, becomes a challenge for us wealthier world citizens. It's no wonder Jesus said that it was easier for a camel to pass through the eye of a needle than a rich person to enter the kingdom of God. The hard fact is that it simply is not possible to serve both God and money. It's one or the other.

Poverty, the Blues, and Consumption

We began by thinking about the poverty in which black communities in the Deep South lived in the early decades of the twentieth century as the blues emerged and grew up. Born in 1897 in Texas, Blind Willie Johnson, whom we mentioned briefly in the previous chapter, was one of the most influential of the early bluesmen. Like so many of his fellow blacks and other bluesmen of the period, Willie Johnson was born into poverty and never escaped it throughout his life, despite becoming a recording artist and enjoying some success around the end of the 1920s.

Johnson has the distinction of having one of his songs featured on a special recording sent aboard the Voyager spacecraft, launched in 1977 to head beyond the outer solar system into deep space. The Voyager Golden Records also contains music by Beethoven, Mozart, and Stravinsky. What any other intelligent life in the universe might make of Willie Johnson's

"Dark Was the Night" is anybody's guess. Johnson's life, however, knew little of this sort of success and his life was blighted by the disadvantages that poverty brings.

Willie Johnson wasn't born blind; rather his blindness was likely the result of a tragic, avoidable accident. When Willie was seven, his father beat his stepmother after catching her going out with another man. The stepmother then picked up a handful of lye and threw it, and it hit the face not of Willie's father, but of young Willie. The rest of Johnson's life was no less tragic. Although he had the opportunity to record thirty studio songs for Columbia Records during 1927–1930 and outsold the likes of Bessie Smith with his first 78, *I Know His Blood Can Make Me Whole / Jesus Make Up My Dying Bed,* the Great Depression just about killed Johnson's recording career. He spent his life mostly busking for small change and preaching on street corners. The fact that he was an accomplished guitarist, playing with a rhythmic picking style or sometimes sliding with a brass ring or a knife, such that Eric Clapton could call his playing on "It's Nobody's Fault But Mine" "probably the finest slide guitar playing you'll ever hear," never translated into financial success for him.

Poor all his life, he spent his time preaching and singing in the streets of several Texas cities. Finally, in 1945, his home burned to the ground and Willie ended up living in the burned-out ruins, sleeping on a wet bed in the late summer Texas heat. The result was that he contracted malaria and died before he was fifty, on September 18, 1945. Reports vary but it seems he was refused admission at the hospital either because he was blind or because he was black.

Johnson's was a tragic life, blighted, of course, by the terrible incident as a child when he lost his sight, but also by the circumstances of poverty in which he lived. The Great Depression of 1929 hit poor blacks in the South very badly indeed and this, combined with the injustice of the Jim Crow era and his disability, confined Willie to a life of lack.[23]

Johnson, however, had a strong Christian faith and was one of the first to articulate what became a strong strand in the history of the blues— gospel blues. His song "If I Had My Way I'd Tear The Building Down" landed him in jail—apparently he was busking in front of a customshouse and it was thought he was using the song lyrics to try to provoke a riot. The song, of course, is a spirited retelling of the biblical story of Samson and Delilah.

23. Oakley, *The Devil's Music*, 145ff.

In "God Don't Never Change" and "Keep Your Lamps Trimmed and Burning," Willie testifies to the faithfulness of God; in "Praise God I'm Satisfied," he takes comfort in his Savior finding him and being a child of God; in "Latter Rain," he celebrates the experience of the Holy Spirit; and in "Jesus is Coming Soon," "I'm Gonna Run to the City of Refuge" and "Bye and Bye I'm Goin' to See the King," he looks forward to participating in God's new day. His life may have been hard and full of trouble due to his blindness and poverty, but Willie Johnson discovered the reality of a faith that was truly, for him, good news.

Willie Johnson, although a talented musician and songwriter, did not have the opportunity to turn his talent into wealth and status. He discovered, however, that there was something in life that is truly more important than these—a trust in the faithfulness of God. Willie Johnson's songs have endured the test of time and have been covered over the decades by many blues artists and bands, keeping alive his legacy of a simple trust in God, despite the difficult circumstance of life.

More recently, Walter Trout, who has played with Canned Heat and John Mayall's Bluesbreakers, and who is one of the world's outstanding electric blues guitarists, released an album entitled *Blues for the Modern Daze*. On it he reacts to the oppressive pressure of the modern world on us to earn more and consume more. In "Turn Off Your TV," he resists the urgent messages of the advertising industry:

> They got the latest info
> On what you need to wear
> How to lose a hundred pounds and be a millionaire
> To be all you can be
> Turn off your TV.

The same message comes across in "Puppet Master," and then in "Money Rules the World":

> They're trying to say to me and you
> Corporations are people too
> The way it seems to me, they're trying to steal our democracy . . .
> But it's money, it's money that rules the world.

And then, in the hard-hitting title track, he bemoans the individualism and isolationism that marks our society and the fact that there is so little generosity:

> You'll get yours
> I'll get mine
> It's all for one and none for all . . .
> Ain't nothing left to give
> These times in which we live
> It's dog-eat-dog
> In the modern daze.

Trout's searing guitar solos emphasize the keen edge of his critique of the modern world. They point to the anxious, worrisome, acquisition-hungry spirit of the age and send us thirsting for an alternative, where our humanity can once again flourish. We begin to realize the tyranny of the never-ending search for "more," and Jesus's picture of a simple trust in God for the daily provision of food, drink, and clothing and of the trustworthiness of God begins to become very attractive. We need to shake ourselves from Trout's "modern daze," let the scales fall from our eyes, and realize that the constant pursuit of wealth and goods is but a deception. "Stop worrying about tomorrow," says Jesus. Rather, "set your hearts on God's kingdom first, and on his saving justice, and all these other things will be given you as well."

Listening Guide

Eric Clapton, *Unplugged,* Warner, 1992

J. B. Lenoir, *Vietnam Blues: The Complete L&R Recording,* Evidence, 1999

Mississippi Fred McDowell, *Amazing Grace & My Home Is In The Delta,* Floating World, 2013

Blind Willie Johnson, *Dark Was the Night,* Sony, 1998

seven

The Gospel, the Blues, and the Empire

If anyone forces you to go one mile,
go also the second mile.

MATTHEW 5:41

Go the Extra Mile

We've already explored how Jesus taught radical enemy love as an integral part of discipleship. In the Sermon on the Mount, right after saying we should turn the other cheek when slapped, and before he sums up what he means by "love your enemies and pray for those who harass you," Jesus tells his disciples that "When they force you to go one mile, go with them two." The "they" that Jesus is referring to here is the occupying army of Roman soldiers. The code for Roman soldiers was that they could conscript the local population to carry their kit bags for one mile only.[1] For an occupied people, being forced to do this was bad enough. Jesus, however, says that his followers should offer to go an extra mile.

The interpretation that is usually given to this is that Jesus is advocating nonresistance to evil. Theologian Walter Wink, however, disagrees and suggests that Jesus here is counseling nonviolent resistance. He points out that the Greek word used for "oppose" or "resist" in 5:39, when Jesus says, "You must not oppose those who want to hurt you," literally means to "stand against" and is most often used in the Greek version of the Old

1. France, *The Gospel of Matthew*, 221.

91

Testament as a technical term for warfare. We might expect Matthew to use the word in the same way. So what Jesus is saying here is that his disciples should not "stand against" or engage in warfare against the oppressor. The same word is used in Ephesians 6:13 in Paul's imagery of "withstanding" in the "evil day"—i.e., of "soldiers standing their ground and refusing to flee."[2]

Jesus is not, then, counseling passive submission to oppression and injustice—he is simply saying that a violent, militaristic response is not the way for his followers. Warren Carter gives the sense of the saying: "Don't *violently* resist the one who is evil."[3]

Wink then follows up this interpretation of the text by examining the instructions that follow—"turn the other cheek" and "go the extra mile"—by showing how each of these can be construed as active resistance, albeit nonviolent. He explains that offering the other cheek—i.e., the left cheek—when someone has slapped you on the right cheek should be construed as an act of defiance, because the usual way of a superior slapping an inferior on the right cheek is with the back of the right hand. If the left cheek is offered, the superior then finds it difficult to slap again with the right hand. Wink explains, "The backhand was not a blow to injure, but to insult, humiliate, degrade. It was not administered to an equal, but to an inferior." If the left cheek was then offered, the only feasible way of striking again was with the fist, which was reserved for fighting an equal. And, "the last thing the master wishes to do is to establish this underling's equality," says Wink. So, it seems, that the offering of the left cheek was, in fact, an act of defiance, of asserting one's dignity in the face of oppression. "In that world of honor and shaming, the 'superior' has been rendered impotent to instill shame in a subordinate. He has been stripped of his power to dehumanize the other."[4]

Similarly, when Jesus talks about "going the extra mile," there is more here than simply doing a bit more than is expected of you. The context is the occupation of Palestine in Jesus's day by the Roman Empire, and the way that citizens could be pressed to carry a soldier's heavy pack if required to. The military codes only allowed a one-mile carry, and for a soldier to force a citizen to do more was to risk the discipline of the centurion. Wink makes the case that, by insisting on carrying the pack another mile, the citizen was seizing the initiative from the oppressor—"they have thrown the soldier off balance by depriving him of the predictability of his victim's

2. Wink, *The Powers that Be*, 98.

3. Carter, *Matthew and the Margins*, 151.

4. Wink, *The Powers that Be*, 99.

response." Wink's view is that Jesus's instruction here is not about piety or kindness. Rather, "he is helping an oppressed people find a way to protest and neutralize an onerous practice despised throughout the empire. He is not giving a nonpolitical message of spiritual world transcendence. He is formulating a worldly spirituality in which the people at the bottom of society or under the thumb of imperial power learn to recover their humanity."[5]

Jesus here is advocating neither passive acceptance of injustice and tyranny, nor violent revolt against it—it is a third way of active, nonviolent resistance that asserts human dignity in the face of oppression.

This saying in the Sermon is only one aspect of what Jesus and the New Testament writers have to say about the relationship between the gospel and the powers that be—as we shall see.

The Blues Against the Empire

We have seen how the blues emerged in the context of the oppression and suffering of black people in the Southern US, and that singing the blues was a means of responding to that oppression—of giving voice to great sorrow, lamenting the current state of affairs, but also of expressing dignity in the face of injustice. The blues were also a means of protest against this injustice.

Given the huge inequality that existed, and the whole structuring of society under Jim Crow, it would have been impossible for blues artists to sing protest songs in the way that they were sung in the 1960s when the civil rights movement had gathered momentum. Consequently, often the protest was coded, though sometimes it broke through the surface quite clearly. Although the majority of blues songs are about the troubles of love, there is a steady stream of social protest from the early days right through to the present.

In 1930, Leadbelly recorded a song entitled simply "Jim Crow," in which he bemoans the state of affairs facing him every day of his life, everywhere he goes:

> I been traveling, I been traveling from shore to shore
> Everywhere I have been I find some old Jim Crow.

He can't get away from the racial discrimination he faces—it's there even when he goes to the cinema to be entertained:

5. Ibid., 108.

> I want to tell you people something that you don't know
> It's a lotta Jim Crow in a moving picture show.

And finally he pleads with his hearers, "Please get together, break up this old Jim Crow."

In the early 1930s, nine black teenagers from Scottsboro, Alabama were accused of raping two white women aboard a train. The case highlighted the racism of the Jim Crow system and the injustice of the entire Southern legal system. In a series of trials and retrials, which were rushed and adjudicated by all-white juries and racially biased judges, the nine boys suffered incarceration in the brutally harsh Kilby Prison in Alabama, as well as attempted lynching and mob violence. After three trials, during which one of the young white women who was alleged to be a victim had confessed to fabricating her rape story, five of the nine were convicted and received sentences ranging from seventy-five years imprisonment to death. The one who received the death sentence subsequently escaped, went into hiding and was eventually pardoned by George Wallace in 1976. The case was a landmark and led eventually to the end of all-white juries in the South.

Leadbelly recorded "Scottsboro Boys" in 1938, in which he warns black people not to go to Alabama lest they suffer the same fate as the Scottsboro nine:

> I'm gonna tell all the colored people
> Even the old nigger here
> Don't ya ever go to Alabama
> And try to live.

Leadbelly was clearly not afraid to voice his protest against what he experienced. He also wrote "Bourgeois Blues," perhaps the most famous example of 1930s blues protest songs. Leadbelly here sings about his experience of discrimination in the nation's capital city:

> Well, them white folks in Washington they know how
> To call a colored man a nigger just to see him bow
> Lord, it's a bourgeois town
> I got the bourgeois blues
> Gonna spread the news all around.

Leadbelly talks about looking for accommodation and being turned away by the white landlord:

> Well, me and my wife we were standing upstairs
> We heard the white man say "I don't want no niggers up there."

America, according to Leadbelly may have been hailed as "The home of the Brave, The land of the Free," but it was just somewhere where he was "mistreated" by the "bourgeoisie."

As we've mentioned already, the Great Depression hit black communities in the South particularly hard. Skip James's 1931 "Hard Time Killing Floor Blues" captures the grim reality of the time for many people, with James's high eerie voice and his D-minor-tuned guitar. "The people are drifting from door to door" and they "can't find no heaven."

> Hard time's is here
> An ev'rywhere you go
> Times are harder
> Than th'ever been befo'.

The Great Depression exacerbated the already grim economy in the coalfields in Harlan County, Kentucky, affecting whites as well as blacks. By the end of 1931, more than a third of miners were out of work, and those that had work made as little as 80 cents a day and could only get a few days' work a month. Aunt Molly Jackson used her music to protest eloquently about the dire situation that existed for the miners. She wrote of her experience of seeing starving, barefooted children in "Ragged Hungry Blues" and said she had to "sing out my blues. This song comes from the heart and not just from the point of a pen."

> I woke up this morning, with the worst blues I ever had in my life;
> Not a bite to eat for breakfast, a poor coal miner's wife!
>
> All the women in the coal camps are sitting with bowed down heads,
> Ragged and barefooted, and the children cryin' for bread.
>
> No food, no clothes for our children, I'm sure this head don't lie;
> If we can't get more for our labor we'll starve to death and die!
>
> Some coal operators might tell you the hungry blues are not there.
> They're the worst kind of blues this poor woman ever had.

One of the blues artists who was most articulate about civil rights during this period was Josh White, who was born in 1914 and recorded under the names "Pinewood Tom" and "Tippy Barton" in the 1930s. He became a well-known race record artist during the 1920s and 1930s, moving to New York in 1931 and expanding his repertoire to include not only blues but jazz and folk songs. In addition he became a successful actor on radio, the stage, and film. White was outspoken about segregation and human rights and was suspected of being a communist in the McCarthy era of the early 1950s.

In 1941 he released one of his most influential albums, *Southern Exposure: An Album of Jim Crow Blues*. The title track pulls no punches:

> Well, I work all the week in the blazin' sun,
> Can't buy my shoes, Lord, when my payday comes
> I ain't treated no better than a mountain goat,
> Boss takes my crop and the poll takes my vote.

The album consists mostly of twelve-bar blues songs, including "Jim Crow Train," "Bad Housing Blues," and "Defense Factory Blues." White attacks wartime factory segregation in the latter with, "I'll tell you one thing, that bossman ain't my friend, If he was, he'd give me some democracy to defend." In "Jim Crow Train," he addresses the segregation on the railways:

> Stop the train so I can ride this train.
> Stop Jim Crow so I can ride this train.
> Stop Jim Crow so I can ride this train.
> Black and White folks ridin' side by side.
>
> Damn that Jim Crow.

On White's 1940 "Trouble," he leaves no doubt about the cause of black people's problems: "Well, I always been in trouble, 'cause I'm a black-skinned man." The rest of the song deals with the failed justice system of the time and the inhumane conditions that black inmates suffered when incarcerated:

> Wearin' cold iron shackles from my head down to my knee
> And that mean old keeper, he's all time kickin' me.

As a black man under Jim Crow, all White could expect from life was "Trouble, trouble, makes me weep and moan, Trouble, trouble, ever since I was born."

Big Bill Broonzy was one of the most popular and important of the pre–World War II blues singers, who recorded over 250 songs from 1925 to 1952, including "Key to the Highway," "Black, Brown, and White," "Glory of Love," and "When Will I Get to Be Called a Man." He was a very talented musician, songwriter, and singer, who Eric Clapton said was a role model for him in playing the acoustic guitar. Broonzy claims in his autobiography that he joined the army sometime after 1917 and fought in World War I in France, and on returning to the South he found conditions there quite intolerable. A more recent biography of Broonzy questions his story of joining up, but there can be no doubting the injustice that Broonzy encountered as a black man in the South. He refers to the way in which black men were referred to disparagingly as "boy" by whites in his 1951 song "I Wonder When I'll Be Called a Man."

> When I was born into this world, this is what happened to me
> I was never called a man, and now I'm fifty-three
> I wonder when . . . I wonder when will I get to be called a man
> Do I have to wait till I get ninety-three?

"Black, Brown and White," recorded in 1951, rails against the discrimination that Broonzy found everywhere, be it getting a drink at a bar, being paid less money for doing the same job, or even just getting a job:

> They says if you was white, should be all right
> If you was brown, stick around
> But as you's black, m-mm brother, git back git back git back.

Muddy Waters, the most famous of the Chicago blues artists, also highlighted the patriarchal attitudes of whites to blacks in his 1955 release "Mannish Boy," which on the surface is a rather sensual blues song declaring, "I'm a natural born lover's man," and "I'm a hoochie coochie man." (The hoochie coochie was a sexually provocative dance that became wildly popular in Chicago in the late nineteenth century. The dance was performed by women, so a "hoochie coochie man" either watched them or ran the show.) In the context of a black man never being recognized as anything other than a "boy," however, the song asserts black manhood in the face of white suppression. "I'm a man, I'm a full grown man," sings Muddy, "I spell M-A, child, N"

Bo Diddley's "I'm a Man," again a raunchy R&B hit in the 1950s, with lines like "All you pretty women, Stand in line, I can make love to you baby, In an hour's time," nevertheless is an assertion of manhood against the prevailing attitudes of the time, particularly in Diddley's home state of Mississippi. Again we get the assertion, "I'm a man, I spell M-A-N, man."

Another major and influential blues artist from Mississippi was John Lee Hooker, son of a sharecropper, who came to prominence in the late 1940s and 1950s. His "House Rent Boogie" from 1956 protests the all-too-familiar tale for black Americans of losing a job and not being able to make the rent payment: "I said fellows, never go behind your rent, 'cause if you did it, it will hard so it's cold in the street."

The wail of protest in the blues continued on into that decade most associated with protest songs, the 1960s. From 1961 we have the guitar-harmonica duo of Sonny Terry and Brownie McGhee singing "Keep on Walkin'," which takes up again the theme of blacks being worked hard for little pay:

> The bossman was so mean, you know, I worked just like a slave
> Sixteen long hours drive you in your grave
> That's why I'm walkin', walkin' my blues away.

And then in 1966 we have "Vietnam Blues" by yet another Mississippian, J. B. Lenoir. Drawing an elegant parallel between the US's presence in Southeast Asia and the Jim Crow South, Lenoir demanded of President Lyndon Johnson, "How can you tell the world we need peace, and you still mistreat and killin' poor me?" Lenoir came to Chicago and became an important part of the blues scene there in the 1950s, performing with Memphis Minnie and Muddy Waters. He was a fine singer and a great showman, sporting zebra-striped costumes and nifty electric guitar licks. But Lenoir composed a number of political blues songs bringing sharp social commentary to bear on events going on around him. Songs like "Born Dead," which decries the fact that "Every black child born in Mississippi, you know the poor child is born dead," referring to the lack of opportunity in his home state; or "Eisenhower Blues," which complains that the government had "Taken all my money, to pay the tax." Lenoir also composed the haunting "Down in Mississippi," which he performed on his 1966 *Alabama Blues*. "Down in Mississippi where I was born, Down in Mississippi where I come from," sings Lenoir,

> They had a huntin' season on a rabbit
> If you shoot him you went to jail.
> The season was always open on me:
> Nobody needed no bail.

He concludes about the place of his birth, "I count myself a lucky man, Just to get away with my life." The definitive version of the song, however, was to come some forty years later, when Mavis Staples recorded it on her album *We'll Never Turn Back*. Staples added a little to the song about segregated water fountains and washeterias and how "Dr. King saw that every one of those signs got taken down, down in Mississippi."

Mavis Staples had already made her protest against three hundred years of injustice in 1970 with the no-punches-pulled "When Will We

Be Paid?" The song demanded an answer to the exploitation of black Americans in the construction of America's roads and railroads, in the domestic chores their women have done, and the wars in which their men have fought. Despite this contribution to the making of America, all the remuneration Staples's people got was being "beat up, called names, shot down and stoned." "We have given our sweat and all our tears," she sings, so, "When will we be paid for the work we've done?"

In a similar vein, complaining about the discrimination they faced, Sonny Terry, Brownie McGhee, and Earl Hooker in "Tell Me Why" in 1969 sang,

> Every war that's been won, we helped to fight
> Why in the world can't we have some human rights?
> Tell me why?

They give the cruel answer themselves—"It's got to be my skin, that people don't like."

The steady thread of protest in the blues has continued from then, with Herman E. Johnson's 1973 "Depression Blues" through to recent releases from Robert Cray and Walter Trout protesting about the banking scandals from 2008 onwards, Otis Taylor's protest against slavery (sadly still a blight in our modern world) in "Ten Million Slaves," and antiwar songs from Caroline Wonderland ("God Only Knows"), Candeye Kane ("Jesus and Mohammed"), Doug MacLeod ("Dubb's Talkin' Politician Blues"), and Eddie Clearwater ("Time for Peace").

The Gospel and the Empire

This thread of protest that we have traced in the blues from its earliest days is a cry against injustice, a rallying call to assert human dignity in the face of oppression. It is an outraged cry against a system of domination, with the insight of a suffering people that things should and can be different. The "empire," in whatever guise it takes, in whatever time or place, as an unholy system of domination and oppression, will never have the last word.

When we turn to examine the Christian gospel, we find that it has a great deal to say about justice and the dominating power of the "empire," and about the possibilities and the hope of human freedom. We have seen a glimpse of this already in considering Jesus's talk about going the extra mile or turning the other cheek as an assertion of human dignity in the face of tyranny.

As we have noted, the gospel is much more than personal salvation, important as that is. It is nothing less than the reclamation of God's world by God, the arrival of God's reign to supplant all other sovereignties and claims on human allegiance. It is summed up in the phrase "the kingdom of God," which was the essence of Jesus's message and the focus of early church preaching. By virtue of God raising Jesus from the dead, the first Christians saw that God indeed had decisively entered history in the person of Jesus the Messiah, who was now enthroned in the central place of power in the universe. Their acclamation of the risen Messiah was summed up in the phrase, Jesus is Lord.

In the first chapter of the letter to the Christians at Colossae, Paul explains that the Messiah has been exalted to the highest echelon of power in the universe and that every other power—"whether thrones or dominions or rulers or authorities"—was not only created by him by also "for" him (Col 1:16). In a similar vein, in the Ephesian letter, the author says that the Messiah is "far above all rule and authority and power and dominion" (Eph 1:20).

There has often been a tendency among modern Christians to see these sort of ideas in some sort of "spiritual" sense, relegating Christ's reign to our personal lives and the ongoing struggles we face with sin or, perhaps, evil powers. It can be hard to see beyond this, when religion in our day is seen as something inner, something personal or, at the most, if it has to do with society at all, its primary concern is with sexual mores. We like to keep our religion and politics separate. But the New Testament writers had a much more expansive sense of what the confession "Jesus is Lord" means.

Coming from a Jewish tradition, the New Testament writers' sense of their God was that God was the creator God, the sovereign Lord of the universe before whom all earthly knees, rulers and subjects alike, must bow (e.g., Isaiah 45:3). The rulership of Yahweh meant the reign of Israel's God here on earth, a very tangible here-and-now reality. As we have seen, the Jewish prophets pointed towards a day when Yahweh would return to Zion and establish a new day of his peaceful reign, in the process subduing his enemies. And as we have also seen, the first Christians believed that through the life, death, and resurrection of Jesus, that day had begun.

Tom Wright suggests that "the entire story of Israel, on one level at least, is the story of how Israel's God is taking on the arrogant tyrants of the world, overthrowing their power, and rescuing his people from under its cruel weight."[6] He traces through the Old Testament the ways in which God confronts the powers of empire and evil in the world, rescuing his people at various stages in their history, most notably in the exodus story, and how the hope persists among them, even in the experience of defeat and exile, of the sovereignty of God that will ultimately triumph over wickedness, violence, and domination.

At times this idea is expressed in a sharp critique of pagan empire in Jewish literature, both in the biblical prophets like Isaiah, Jeremiah, and Daniel, and in various other Second Temple texts like those from Qumran. The Book of Daniel is a particularly important text in this regard, with stories of world rulers like Nebuchadnezzar and Cyrus being mere instruments in Yahweh's hand, and Daniel's vision of the four wicked kingdoms rising up and being overthrown and an everlasting government being given to the "Most High" and his people. The Old Testament portrayal of the out-working of God's purposes in the world includes the idea that the rulers of the world are answerable to God and that ultimately God will judge the Pharaohs and the Babylons of the world. For Jews of the first century, then, the idea of God as king was something with real-world significance—politically, socially, and in every way conceivable. The Jewish scriptures, if you like, gave a loud protest against evil and injustice and declared that the powers will not ultimately stand in the face of Yahweh's sovereign rule.

We only have to look again at Israel's blues songbook, the Psalms, to hear the ancient Jewish protest song loud and clear. The ancient Israelites howled in protest against the "wicked" and their "enemies," whether personal or national, remonstrating against their violence, unjust court cases, and hatred. They appealed to God for protection from the wealthy whose abundance came from cheating (Ps 49:5), mocked the arrogance of people with wealth (Ps 49:12), and announced the futility of trust in riches (Ps 49:17).

Israel's prophets, of course, are supreme examples of people who, at great personal cost and danger, called out the political rulers and nobility and wealthy of their day for their unjust practices and their oppression of the poor. They weren't afraid of making a scene; they didn't settle for a comfortable life—they raised their voices in loud protest. Jerusalem, the capital city and the seat of power, was a whore, full of murders, proclaimed Isaiah (Isa 1:21); Hosea exposed fraudulent merchants in the marketplace with their cheating scales (Hos 12:7); Amos roared at Israel's leaders who, he

6. Wright, *When God Became King*, 129

said, twisted "justice, making it a bitter pill for the oppressed" (Amos 5:7); and Micah pointed the finger squarely at his country's political leadership as he accused it of "tearing the skin from off my people and their flesh from off their bones" (Mic 3:2).

This is the heritage of understanding of Yahweh's rule that Jesus and his first followers inherited—it was rich in social protest against injustice and oppression. Because God's people knew that this state of affairs was the very opposite of God's purpose for God's world.

The Roman Empire

In the first century AD during Jesus's lifetime and the emergence of the Christian church, the global superpower was Rome. The Roman Empire swept from Cappadocia in the east across the Mediterranean world to Spain in the west. It included North Africa in the south up to Britain in the north. Many of us associate the Romans with building roads, waterways, and giving the world the basis of a legal system, but the reality was that Rome was a totalitarian regime, which expanded its empire through violence and ruled through the threat of violence. Taxation was exacted from conquered peoples, Roman law imposed, and criminals and would-be freedom fighters were executed publicly by the brutal method of crucifixion.

The first emperor, Augustus, came to power in 27 BC after subduing his enemies. He effectively was able to vest all power in himself, eventually becoming *pontifex maximus*, the high priest of the collegium of the pontifices, the most important position in Roman religion. He claimed the title *pater patriae*, or "father of the country." Augustus was deified by the Senate upon his death in 14 AD, and the cult of *Divus Augustus* continued as the state religion of the Empire until 391 AD.

The belief of the Roman emperors and the expectation of many of Rome's citizens was that it was Rome's destiny to enjoy material blessings on earth—fertility and crops, peace, stability and order, abundance and tranquility. All this came through the Roman emperor, who was put forth as the "savior," guided and blessed by the gods. The gods gave him military victory and the ability to subdue and dominate other people groups. He brought "peace" (*pax*) and "justice" (*iustitia*) to the world—by the required level of violence, of course.

The costs of conquest were borne by the vast majority of the inhabitants of the empire—the slaves, peasants, and laborers who actually produced the wealth that was enjoyed by a small circle of wealthy and powerful individuals. Violence and force were the methods employed by the Empire—in conquest and in keeping order. Said one senator in 61 AD, "It is only by terror you can hold in such a motley rabble."[7] The Roman lawyer and senator Cicero said, "Dominion has been granted by Nature to everything that is best, to the great advantage of what is weak."[8] It was, said the Roman poet Virgil (in his myth of the founding of Rome, the *Aeneid*), the destiny of the Romans to "crush warrior nations," to "have dominion without end . . . to crown peace with justice."[9]

The expression for the reciprocal relationship between the Roman imperial order and the conquered peoples was *fides*—"faithfulness." Cicero hailed justice (*ius*) and faithfulness (*fides*) as the hallmarks of beneficent Roman rule. These were all, of course, euphemisms for the required subjection and willing obedience required by Rome. Emperor Augustus himself said "a large number of nations experienced the good faith of the Roman people (*fides*) and through him [Augustus] the Roman people themselves came in their divinely ordained destiny, to rule the world."[10]

Augustus was believed to have saved the world from itself, to have ended warfare and brought order to the world. Not surprisingly, his successors often deliberately emphasized the continuity between their own reign and that of Augustus. The dominion of Rome in the world was emphasized to the empire's citizenry in a number of ways, including the grand city architecture, coins with their inscriptions stressing peace and happiness, and literature.

In addition, in the early part of the first century, the cult of Caesar, in which the Roman emperor was proclaimed and honored as divine, had become dominant in a large part of the Empire, particularly in the East. This, along with force, coercion, and violence, was one of the ways in which the Romans managed to control and govern huge areas of the Mediterranean world. Price suggests that "the imperial cult was a major part of the web of power that formed the fabric of society."[11] The cult was not about meaningless honors given to Caesar; instead, it was about using symbols to show how local populations fitted in to the new order of the reality of Rome. The

---

7. So said the Roman lawyer, Gaius Cassius, quoted in Tacitus, *Ann.* XIV, 44–45.

8. Cicero, *De re publica*, 3:37.

9. Virgil, *The Aeneid*, Book 1.

10. *Res Gestae Divi Augusti*, 32.

11. Price, *Rituals and Power*, 248.

reality of the empire and its domination over daily life was ever present in the Mediterranean world of the first century.

Jesus and Empire

In Jesus's time, Palestine was occupied by the Romans and their vassal rulers, the Herodians. The fortresses sited near Jerusalem (at Herodium and Hyrcania) and throughout Palestine declared loudly and clearly that Rome was in control, even though there may not have been much sign of Roman legionaries in the towns and cities. Though generally Roman rule was somewhat muted in Palestine, people were aware that the Romans were more than capable of ruthless suppression of any dissent. Various rebellions were put down callously on Herod the Great's death around 4 BC. Older people could remember the scenes of bloody slaughter. And the Romans were again to show the efficiency of their military machine during the Jewish rebellion of 70 AD, when they destroyed the temple and Jerusalem. Rome, and the threat of Rome, was ever present during Jesus's lifetime. Alan Storkey suggests that Jewish culture at the time was shaped by "military victory and dominance," and the cruelty and viciousness of conquest and reconquest was "the underlying system of legitimation."[12]

How much, then, we might ask, was there a note of protest against the power of empire in Jesus's life and ministry? First of all, Jesus was a Jew who was a faithful reader of his people's scriptures and who knew the traditions of hope for a new day of God's peaceful rule on earth, and of prophetic protest against oppression and injustice.

At the beginning of his ministry, Luke records Jesus reading in the synagogue from Isaiah 61:

> The Spirit of the Lord is on me, because he has anointed me to proclaim good news to the poor. He has sent me to proclaim freedom for the prisoners and recovery of sight for the blind, to set the oppressed free, to proclaim the year of the Lord's favor. (Luke 4:18–19, NRSV)

Here Jesus sets out his stall as one standing firmly in the line of Israel's prophets who cry "enough!" The rule of God, which he realized was being inaugurated through himself, was entirely different from the rule of the Herodians or the Romans, which was based on naked power and aggression. The rule of God called for a transformation in the relationships in

12. Storkey, *Jesus and Politics*, 41.

the world—now down was up, up was down, the poor were lifted up and the tyrants and dictators of the world were living on borrowed time. The gospel writers record for us Jesus, before the beginning of his ministry, being tempted by the devil in the wilderness. In the temptations we see Jesus repudiate "national glory and the human quest for power and domination over others as not God's way, as not worthy of consideration."[13] This approach was to be the hallmark of his ministry.

Jesus's conception of the kingdom of God of necessity brought him into conflict with the powers that be—and of course he was eventually executed as a political rebel as the "king of the Jews" by Rome. The rule of God, for Jesus, meant that all human rulers and politics were effectively dethroned and given a subservient place.

The three synoptic Gospels record for us Jesus being questioned by the Jerusalem leadership, which was allied with Rome. In their accounts, Jesus has just undertaken the prophetic action of cleansing the headquarters of Jewish political, economic, and religious power, the temple, and the Jewish leadership, feeling the threat of Jesus's alternative vision of what God's kingdom looks like, tries to trap him. They use the issue of taxation, which went to the heart of Roman colonial rule—nonpayment of taxes was tantamount to rebellion. They ask Jesus if they should be paying taxes or not. Warren Carter takes the view that, in answering, Jesus "cleverly combines loyalty and deference with his own subversive agenda. He employs ambiguous, coded, and self-protective speech to uphold payment of a coin bearing the emperor's image while also asserting overriding loyalty to God."[14] Jesus says that Jews should pay the tax due—literally, "give back" Caesar's coin to him—coins which, bearing Caesar's image, most Jews would have considered blasphemous. It's all that is owed to Caesar. To Israel's God, however, what belongs to him—God's people, their land, in fact everything in the world—is to be given to him.[15] What sounds on the surface like a rather compliant response by Jesus is actually "a disguised, dignity-restoring act of resistance that recognizes God's all encompassing claim."[16]

Jesus's understanding of the sovereignty of Israel's God meant that all earthly rulers, including the emperor, were subservient to God. Rome was put in its true place and Jesus's followers were told not to fear rulers and

13. Storkey, *Jesus and Politics*, 79.

14. Carter, *The Roman Empire and the New Testament*, 29.

15. Psalm 50:10ff. Yahweh claims that "the world is mine, and all that is in it."

16. Carter, *The Roman Empire and the New Testament*, 29.

only to fear God (Matt 10:28). "Jesus deconstructs ruler- and state-centered cultures and opens up the truth that human beings live first before God, who has created them and not as animals of the state."[17]

Such a stance, of course, is never welcomed by human regimes, which are hungry for power and thrive on domination. The values of the alternative way of being human which Jesus saw was integral to living under God's rule, and which he instructed his followers about in the Sermon on the Mount, were diametrically opposed to the way in which Rome functioned. Love, including enemy love, replaced violence and self-serving; peacemaking replaced war and the threat of war; meekness replaced self-assertion and self-promotion; and a thirst for justice replaced all forms of oppression.

Such a way of being God's people and being human called to account the Jewish leadership of Jesus's day, which was hopelessly compromised in its relationship with Rome—and, as well, the positions of some of his compatriots who were committed to using violence to drive out the pagan oppressors. Ultimately it was not to be tolerated, and Jesus was delivered to the empire so that it could do what empires normally do when faced with perceived troublemakers—it tortured and executed him.

Paul and Empire

As we have already seen, the good news that Paul and the other first Christians preached was the same good news that Jesus preached—it was that the new day of God's government had arrived through the life, death, and resurrection of the Messiah. Paul, having himself met the risen Jesus, was convinced that Jesus had been exalted to the highest position in the universe and that he was "Lord." Paul uses the same Greek word to describe Jesus as his Greek Bible used to describe Israel's God, Yahweh. The Jewish "Lord," Yahweh, for Jews was the creator God, the giver of life and the one who held together and ruled the whole universe. Paul now includes Jesus within his understanding of the divine identity.[18]

As such, the confession "Jesus is Lord" for Paul and the early Christians was foundational. It expressed both their understanding of who Jesus

17. Storkey, *Jesus and Politics*, 126.

18. As Romans 9:5 makes clear—"To them belong the patriarchs, and from their race, according to the flesh, is the Christ, who is God over all, blessed forever." Also Colossians 1:15. Wright, *The Climax of the Covenant*, 93–94: "Paul credits Jesus with a rank and honour which is . . . the rank and honour explicitly reserved, according to scripture, for Israel's God and him alone." See also Bauckham, *God Crucified*.

was and their understanding of the structure of the world. Paul uses the word "Lord" in reference to Jesus over 250 times in the letters ascribed to him in the New Testament. For Paul, a confession of allegiance to the Lord Jesus, along with a belief in his resurrection, brought salvation (Rom 10:9); Christ is the Lord of the living and the dead (Rom 14:9); and is the one to whom every knee will bow and every tongue confess (Rom 14:10 and Phil 2:10–11); and he is the one "through whom and for whom all things exist (1 Cor 8:6 and Col 1:16).

Confessing Jesus is Lord, for Paul, was not, then, some sort of personalized, interior idea of Christ being Lord in one's heart—in the context of the kingdom of God and the Jewish sense of who God is, it means that Jesus really is Lord of the whole here-and-now, tangible world. And crucially, in Paul's historical context, if Jesus was Lord, then Caesar was *not* Lord. Wright has said of Paul's mission that it was that

> of an ambassador for a king-in-waiting, establishing cells of people loyal to this new king, and ordering their lives according to his story, his symbols, and his praxis, and their minds according to his truth. This could only be construed as deeply counter-imperial, as subversive to the whole edifice of the Roman Empire; and there is in fact plenty of evidence that Paul intended it to be so construed, and that when he ended up in prison as a result of his work he took it as a sign that he had been doing his job properly.[19]

In a context where the emperor was hailed as the "son of God" and "savior," proclaimed "peace" and "justice" to his subjects, and propagated the "good news" of gospel of the blessings of Rome's rule, Paul's alternative proclamation of a crucified Jewish royal pretender uses very much the same sort of terms, and could not have been heard as anything else by the citizens of the empire but as a challenge to the pagan ordering of the world. At the very beginning of Paul's letter to Jesus followers who were living in the capital of the empire, Paul's description of the Messiah Jesus includes these terms, which were used of the emperor for Jesus as the true Lord of the world, who calls for the "obedience" and "loyalty" of the nations to himself.

In Paul's world, dominated by the political reality of Rome, the word *gospel* was used for the celebration of the birth or accession of the emperor. In this context, Paul's gospel was likely heard as a summons to allegiance to another king (Acts 17:17), which is why Paul gets into trouble in the Roman colony of Philippi and winds up in jail, and then eventually ends up

19. Wright, "Paul's Gospel and Caesar's Empire," 161.

in Rome where he is subsequently executed by the Roman regime. Wright suggests a more appropriate way to refer to Paul is "royal herald" rather than preacher or theological teacher.[20]

Later on in his Roman letter (5:1), Paul tells the Christians that it is by faith in, or loyalty to, God's Messiah, that we are put in the right—justified, receiving God's verdict of being among the just. That is the thing that brings peace. (Paul here doubtless is thinking of his Hebrew concept of shalom, as we have seen, a broad concept of well-being and flourishing, of the wholeness of creation in the new age, rather than simply "peace in your heart.") In the center of an empire that proclaimed its accomplishments of world domination by military might, severe taxation, and ruthless enforcement of the *Pax Romana,* Paul speaks of an alternative reality, of a world that is ruled by God, to whom the Roman emperors must answer (Rom 13:2—even they are appointed by God). Jesus brings to the world true peace, real justice, and the hope of glorification.

It doesn't take much imagination to think that Romans who heard Paul's letter read to them would have readily appreciated the contrast between what God was doing in Christ and the circumstances dictated by the Roman emperor. In the face of the pretentions of Rome and a so-called justice that favored the rich and powerful, that established its rule by violence, that maintained this rule by the threat of violence and a fixed system of honour and status, stands the justice of the one true God. Where humility, not posturing, is the key virtue;[21] where everyone—rich and poor alike—is on the same level playing field, sinners in need of the salvation brought by the Messiah (Rom 1 and 2); where even the dirt-poor Christian believer, and not the emperor, has the hope of being "glorified" (Rom 5:2); and where "danger or the sword" or anything else that Caesar's system can throw against you (Rom 8: 34) cannot separate you from God's love shown in the Messiah. According to Romans 5:1, peace and justice—*pax* and *iustitia* in Roman terms—come not through the Lord Nero, but through *our* Lord, Jesus the Messiah. Christians have an alternative Lord who is the true bringer of justice.

The justice of God, then, stands in sharp contrast to the justice of the empire. Paul's Letter to the Romans, built solidly on his Jewish theology and understanding of God's justice, but now focused on and funneled through

20. See Wright's chapter entitled "Gospel and Empire" in Wright, *Paul in Fresh Perspective,* for a good discussion of this.

21. Romans 12:3: "don't think of yourself more highly than you ought."

the Messiah Jesus, sets forth an alternative world view to the one that sought to force its way into the Romans' minds every day. No wonder Paul says in Romans 12:2 "don't be conformed to this world, but be transformed by the renewing of your minds." The vision he sets forth for them in this letter has the potential to rescue them from slavery to the pretensions and expectations of the Empire. Jesus followers around the empire's cities were surrounded by a culture, by architecture, by a way of life that proclaimed the glory of Rome. Paul writes to lift their heads above all this, to see an alternative vision of the way the world really is, of the seismic change there has been because of the resurrection of Jesus and to encourage them that a new way of being human really is possible.

In his letters, then, we find this same note of resistance that we found in Jesus, which declares that, despite injustice, oppression, and exploitation, the world has a new Lord and there is a new way of being human, which ultimately will prevail.

The Blues as a Means of Resistance

The blues provided a means for black Americans to assert their humanity and dignity in the context of an oppressive system that declared they were less than human. Whether the songs expressed explicit protest at this or not (and most blues songs did not), the blues, nevertheless, was black music, and, whether it was complaining about unfaithful lovers or problems with the landlord, whether it was performed as dance music in the juke joint or sung on the street corner, it reflected the abuse and indignities suffered by blacks under Jim Crow. It's for this reason that the blues is distinctly black music. As James Cone put it, the blues contains "the essential ingredients that define the essence of black experience."[22]

So the blues was a means of resistance, a means of facing the oppressor with human dignity intact, no matter about the lynchings, the segregation, the verbal abuse, and the injustice, for saying, as Muddy Waters did, "I'm a man, I spell M-A-N." Willie Dixon gets it spot on when he says "The blues are the true facts of life expressed in words and song, inspiration, feeling, and understanding."[23] In telling the truth about the misery of black experience, but as well as that, a hope for change, the blues was a part of the endurance and resistance of the black community.

22. Cone, *The Spirituals and the Blues*, 102.

23. Dixon with Snowden, *I Am the Blues*, 2.

At least part of the reason for this is that the blues grew out of the spirituals, with their strong sense of God's presence in the midst of suffering and their hope for a better world. The element of resistance against the "empire" that we have discovered is part of the tradition of God's people in the Bible, and is crucial to Christian faith, finds expression in the spirituals with their retelling of the exodus story where the empire in the form of Pharaoh gets its comeuppance, and their assertion of blacks' value in God's eyes. No matter that the blues goes off on its own secular trajectory, these values of self-worth and resistance to the oppressor carry on in the blues.

And, as we have seen, there is a continual thread of explicit protest as well, where the ills and injustice suffered are called out, and where the victims are no longer willing to be victims. In this way, the blues points us toward the reality underlying the protest against the empire.

Christian faith says that there is a reason to hope that the empire's days are numbered and that there really is a power in the world able to overcome its domination. Because Jesus is Lord, there is no other Lord. Those set free by Christ are set free from the dominion of any other power. Communities of believers are communities of resistance to whatever form the empire may take, whether it is outright oppression, or the slow, life-sapping power of consumerism. In these Jesus following groups, people can find encouragement, strength, and the power of God's spirit to stand against the tide of popular culture, against whatever dehumanizing pressures come their way—because they know that something has radically changed in the world, that because of the resurrection of Christ and his exaltation to the highest position in the universe, there is an alternative to living lives dominated by selfishness, violence, addiction, and anxiety.

It is possible to be free from the diktats of the empire; Jesus is Lord, the Spirit is with us and the power of love will prove mightier than all the violent rage in the world. The challenge is to imagine that a new way of life is possible, that a new world is possible; and to live in a way that protests against and challenges the injustice that we see around us. In so much as the blues are a powerful example of the wail of protest of a people against injustice and an assertion of humanity in the face of that injustice, they are a pointer to the protest of the gospel of Jesus Christ against the dehumanizing tendencies of all empires and the assertion of a new humanity that is possible—and only possible—in the Messiah.

Listening Guide

Skip James, *I'd Rather Be The Devil: The Legendary 1931 Session*, Rev-Ola, 2007

Josh White, *Southern Exposure: An Album of Jim Crow Blues*, Flapper, 1997

Sonny Terry & Brownie McGhee, *The Essential . . .* , Primo, 2009

Mavis Staples, *We'll Never Turn Back,* Pinnacle, 2007

Muddy Waters, *Hard Again*, Sony, 2004

eight

The Devil Don't Have No Music

And do not bring us to the time of trial,
but rescue us from the evil one.

MATTHEW 6:1

The Blues and the Devil

The devil is a powerful image in the history of the blues. And the devil is most closely connected to the legend of the crossroads, where the bluesman goes to the crossroads at midnight and, in a Faustian bargain, sells his soul to the devil in return for some instant guitar chops. The legend is mostly, but probably erroneously, connected to Robert Johnson, considered by many to be the greatest of the early Delta bluesmen. Robert Johnson was an exceptional guitarist and singer who recorded only twenty-nine songs and was not well-known during his short life—he was murdered in 1936, in his midtwenties. He was, however, "discovered" by Eric Clapton and The Rolling Stones in the 1960s and since then his name has become revered amongst blues aficionados.

In an interview with NPR in March 2004, when he released an album of Robert Johnson songs in tribute to him, Clapton said that when he first heard Johnson's music as a teenager he was both overwhelmed and also repelled by the intensity of it. Johnson's music was, he said, "so much more powerful than anything else I had heard or was listening to. Amongst all of his peers I felt he was the one that was talking from his soul without really compromising for anybody."[1] Throughout his career, Clapton has been playing electric versions of Johnson's songs, perhaps most famously the song entitled "Crossroad Blues."

Johnson learned to play music on the diddley bow, a makeshift instrument wherein a broom wire or piece of cotton baling wire was stretched between two wires on the side of a house and then the string was plucked and the pitch adjusted by running a piece of metal or glass along it. It was an instrument of poverty, used, often with great skill, to produce a haunting melody in the absence of being able to afford a guitar. As a teenager, Johnson watched Son House and Willie Brown performing, having slipped out of bed late at night, and would try to play their guitars during an interval—much to House's displeasure because he didn't think Johnson's playing was up to much. Johnson then disappeared from Mississippi for around six months to a year, and when he reappeared, he was a confident, strutting young bluesman, handling his guitar "with such speed, facility, and ease that the others [were] left dumbfounded."[2]

It is easy to see how the legend of the crossroads and the devil plays into this turnaround in Johnson's musical performance skills. Add to this some of Johnson's songs—"Hellhound on My Trail," "Me and the Devil Blues," "Preachin' Blues (Up Jumped the Devil)" and "Crossroad Blues"—and there has been plenty to prop up the devil story. And, of course, to further water these particular seeds, there was a Hollywood film in 1988 called *Crossroads*, with a fictional story that featured Robert Johnson, Willie Brown, and a guitar-playing contest with the devil.

The legend, though, is probably better associated with Tommy Johnson—no relation to Robert—whose brother Ledell recounted a story of Tommy selling his soul to the devil at crossroad.[3] Ledell later changed his story so that the setting was a graveyard at midnight![4]

1. Clapton, interviewed by Edwards, "Eric Clapton Takes on Robert Johnson's Blues," *Morning Edition*.

2. Giola, *Delta Blues*, 160.

3. Rev. LeDell Johnson is quoted saying, "Tom said, 'If you want to learn how to play anything you want to play and learn how to make songs yourself, you take your guitar and you go to where a road crosses that way, where a crossroad is. Get there, be sure to get these just a little 'fore twelve o'clock . . . a big black man will walk up there and take your guitar, and he'll tune it. . . . That's the way I learned to play anything I want.'" Ibid., 160–61.

4. Wardlow, *Chasin' That Devil Music*, 197.

Ted Giola, however, in his excellent recent history of the Delta blues, prefers not to dismiss the Robert Johnson link to the story too readily and suggests that Johnson may have spread the story about himself for its notoriety value. He notes the 1992 documentary *The Search for Robert Johnson*, which contains interviews with two people, including a former girlfriend, who knew Johnson, and who said that he spread the crossroads story himself.[5] In addition, a contemporary of Johnson, David "Honeyboy" Edwards, says in his autobiography, "It may be Robert could have sold himself to the devil."[6]

That said, Johnson's song "Crossroad Blues," which in the popular imagination might seem to tie in with the devil pact story, actually has nothing to do with this. The song is about being at the crossroads, trying to "flag a ride," i.e., hitchhike (where better than at a crossroads?) but being unsuccessful. The singer then appeals for help, not to the devil—but actually to the Lord: "Asked the lord above, Have mercy now, save poor Bob if you please." The song goes on to bemoan the fact that the sun is sinking and with it, "poor Bob's" soul. This may be a reference to the danger of a black man being abroad after dark in the South.[7]

Another early bluesman who courted notoriety through an association with the devil was Peattie Wheatstraw, otherwise known as "The Devil's Son-in-Law," or the "High Sheriff from Hell." Wheatstraw's biographer, Paul Garon, reports, decades after Wheatstraw's death, that these titles were the first thing people who knew Wheatstraw said when asked about him.[8]

Wheatstraw was an enormously popular singer during the 1930s and one of the most-recorded blues singers and accompanists. Some of his songs deliberately supported his demonic persona—like "Devil's Son-in-Law," where he boasts of having eleven women, and "Gangster Blues," where he says to a man who's been kissing his wife, " I'm gonna tear you a-pieces and put you back again, I've got the gangster's blues."

Then there was Skip James, who recorded "Devil Got My Woman." Paramount promoted the song with posters showing a cartoon version of James, complete with horns, tail, and a pitchfork. These devil songs were evidently popular and good for business.

---

5. Giola, *Delta Blues*, 163.

6. Edwards et al., *The World Don't Owe Me Nothing*, 105.

7. Palmer, *Deep Blues*, 126.

8. Garon, *Blues and the Poetic Spirit*.

As well as the associations that the blues had with the devil, there was a great deal of superstition in the Delta region, where the blues began. This included the idea of "mojo." Mojo was a fetish or charm, held in a small red flannel bag, that had its roots in West African culture. It was said to drive away evil spirits, give good luck, and to lure and persuade lovers. Muddy Waters, born around 1913 in Mississippi, but who moved to Chicago and became one of the most famous electric bluesmen in the 1950s, made mojo famous with his songs "Louisiana Blues" and "Hootchie Cootchie Man." "Louisiana Blues" was the first successful recording of amplified Delta blues and was Muddy's first nationwide hit in 1950. "I'm goin' down to New Orleans, Get me a mojo hand," sings Muddy. And in "Hootchie Cootchie Man" he elaborates further, "I got a black cat bone, I got a mojo too, I got the John the Conqueroo, I'm gonna mess with you."

Muddy said, "We all believed in mojo hands. You get a mojo, and if you're gamblin' it'll take care of that; you win. If you're after the girls, you can work that on the woman you want and win. Black people really believe in this hoodoo, and the black people in Louisiana was a little more up into that thing than the peoples in the Delta part, as far as makin' things that would work."[9]

Waters recalls his grandparents and their parents all being very superstitious—"they thought people could point their finger at you and make snakes and frogs jump out of you, or make you bark like a dog."[10]

These sorts of ideas in the blues, and their association with juke joints and unsanctified behavior such as drinking and dancing, meant that churchgoing people often, though not always, characterized the blues as the "devil's music." The struggle between the devil and the Lord was often played out in the life of the blues musician. Son House was a case in point. House was one of the original Delta bluesmen and was a convicted murderer, a drinker, and a rambler. But as a young teenager, he was a hard worker in the cotton fields and a passionate churchgoer. By the time he was twenty, he had become pastor of a small Baptist church in Mississippi. His downfall was an older woman, however, with whom he had a fiery affair. He also had an "affair" with the blues—House had a sort of conversion in reverse. One night in 1927, while he was still a pastor, he was out for a walk, and he strolled past a house where a party or "frolic" was taking place. It was here he heard the sound of glass on steel—the bottleneck slide—which

9. Palmer, *Deep Blues,* 96

10. Ibid., 97

he had heard years before, but which now seemed to grip him. He stopped to listen. "Jeez!" he said. "Wonder what's that he's playing? I knew that guitars hadn't usually been sounding like that. So I eases up close enough to look. Sounds good," House said, "Jeez, I like that! I believe I want to play one of them things."[11]

Whereupon he got himself a guitar, albeit with only five strings and a hole in the back. After Willie Wilson (who was the bluesman at the frolic whom he had heard) fixed it up for him, he learned to play it. With his guitar tuned in open G, he soon was "zinging it," as he called it, with the bottleneck slide. Within a matter of weeks, he was out earning money at gigs. And as he said himself, "I kept on playing and got better and better."

House tried to combine his ministry with a career as a gigging bluesman but really, he had decided to dedicate himself to his new profession, and something had to give. His song "Preachin' the Blues"—which became House's signature song and which he performed and recorded for four decades—vividly described the tussle between the church and the blues devils for House's soul, a tussle the church kept losing. He sang:

> Oh and I had religion Lord this very day
> But the womens and whiskey, well they would not let me pray.

House developed a taste for alcohol and women that ultimately made it just too difficult to maintain his ministry as a Baptist preacher, although the final break with his faith did not come for a while yet. The road along which House traveled for the rest of his life was never smooth—he was incarcerated in the notorious Parchman Farm prison for manslaughter, his relationships with women were never straightforward, to say the least, and his drinking descended into alcoholism. His performing career petered out in the early 1940s, although he enjoyed a brief revival towards the end of his life from 1965 on, in the period's folk music revival.

House's preaching career seems to have lasted about seventeen years. By all accounts he was an accomplished preacher. One who heard him, Elizabeth Moore, said "He *really* could sing and he *really* could preach."[12] Yet, probably for most of his preaching career, he was living a double life, drinking and womanizing. It is likely that House was in some inner turmoil living this way. In "Preachin' the Blues," a deacon jumps up in church and accuses the minister:

11. Lester, "I Can Make My Own Songs," 40
12. Quoted in Beaumont, *Preachin' the Blues*, 80.

Another deacon jumped up and said, "Why don't ya hush?"
"You know you drink corn liquor and your life's a horrible stink."

This sounds very like the accusation that House either had thrown at himself or felt should have been thrown at him. Perhaps House knew that he himself was guilty of precisely this sort of hypocrisy.

Son House illustrates the struggle between the devil and the Lord, played out in an individual life. It reminds us of the words of St. Paul in his Letter to the Romans:

> For I know that nothing good dwells within me, that is, in my flesh.
> I can will what is right, but I cannot do it. For I do not do the good
> I want, but the evil I do not want is what I do. (Rom 7:18, 19)

Paul knew that his readers in Rome knew just what he was talking about, because this idea of being torn inside between what you know is right and the way you actually act, had been discussed by various writers in the ancient world—and because it is a nearly universal human experience. All of us are to some degree like Son House, feeling that we are pulled at times in directions that we know aren't good by our desires, emotions, or inner demons. Our lives, in that they reflect the struggle between good and evil, are a reflection of a struggle on a much greater scale that goes on in the world around us.

Evil and the Gospel

In what we know as the Lord's Prayer in Matthew 6, Jesus instructs his followers on how to pray. The prayer has been used by Christians in practically every tradition over the centuries since, and although for many it has become something of a formality and has lost much of its impact, the prayer is an expansive one, and revolves around a vital idea—that of the world-transforming arrival of the kingdom of God.

The prayer asks God that God's rule on earth might come, that God's will should prevail in the same way in which God rules in his own sphere, called "heaven." Jesus's message about the arrival of God's rule had two almost paradoxical ideas in it—on the one hand, it was arriving here and now in his own person and ministry, but on the other, it had yet to come. We find this same sense of the now and not yet of the kingdom elsewhere in the New Testament, indicating that, on the one hand, the first Christians believed that in Jesus's life, death, and resurrection something earth shattering and earth transforming had happened, but that they also looked forward to a day when Jesus's Lordship would be universally acknowledged and all of creation fully redeemed and transformed. This idea comes through quite clearly in Paul's writings, in, for example, Romans 8, where he looks forward to the "groaning" and "corruption" of creation coming to an end at a future time, and in Colossians 1, where he explains that, in due course, "all things" will be reconciled to Christ.

So the prayer beseeches God that this day of transformation and justice would come. And then it goes on to ask God for provision for those that await that day—for "daily bread," and in the light of God's forgiveness, for the grace to forgive those who oppose them. In this, it seems to assume that Jesus's followers who are longing for God's day of transformation to come will anticipate that day by lives that exhibit the values of the kingdom, and will be sustained in this by God's provision—here and now. As we listen to Jesus's teaching in the Sermon, it is clear that he expects his followers to live as if the kingdom had arrived in all its fullness, living out its values and demonstrating the reality that is still fully to come. Many of the things Jesus teaches—radical enemy love, peacemaking, meekness, a refusal to be anxious in the face of all that life throws at you—seem foolhardy; this is just not the way the world works, and to live in such a way seems sure to invite disaster.

This is precisely the point—living in the way that Jesus teaches is out of kilter with the way things presently are, but it coheres completely with the world that is to come and is meant to be a demonstration even now of the reality of the coming kingdom.

In this situation, where disciples are longing for the new world and even now living out the values of that world, they should expect opposition and need to pray for God's strength to overcome it. Jesus has already said that pursuing justice and following him would lead to persecution (5:10, 11). And so in the prayer, after urging God to bring in God's kingdom fully and praying for God's provision to live out the values of the kingdom even now, Jesus says we should pray to be delivered from evil or from the evil one. The Greek used here can be translated in either way.

Jesus, then, is not unrealistic about the state of the world. It was, and still is, beset by evil. Jewish faith was in a Creator who had created a good world—"and God saw that it was good" (Gen 1:10). But the Jewish scriptures very quickly introduce us to the problem of evil, which invaded God's good creation with the disobedience of the first family, the murder of Abel, and the human arrogance that overstretched itself in the story of the tower of Babel. They also, however, begin to tell us the long story of "what God has done, is doing and will do about evil."[13]

That story revolved around the calling of a people who were to be a blessing to the whole world (Gen 12), and then the subsequent failure of this people to live up to their vocation to be the means by which God would undo the evil in God's world. The story, which ended in the sorry experience of exile in Babylon, nevertheless was continued by the hope of Jewish prophets, like Isaiah and Jeremiah, that God would yet bring an end to injustice and bring a completion to God's evil-defeating project. The New Testament is the story of how, surprisingly, the narrative has its completion and fulfilment in the life, death, and resurrection of Jesus the Messiah, who, as Israel's representative, enabled God's purposes for dealing with evil to be brought to a climax.

Wright sums up the Jewish scriptures as "a narrative of God's project of justice within a world of injustice. This project is a matter of setting the existing creation to rights."[14] The way that God did this was through the death and resurrection of Jesus. Although many Christians today highlight substitutionary atonement as the preeminent way in which Jesus's death is to be understood, probably the primary way in which the first Christians interpreted the death and resurrection of Jesus was as a victory over evil. For Paul, in Christ, God had condemned and executed sin (Rom 8:3); all God's enemies were defeated, including, importantly, death (1 Cor 15); all the anti-God, evil powers in the world had been defeated (Col 2:15); and Jesus followers were set free from slavery to their own passions, desires, and the power of sin (Rom 6:18).

There is an overwhelming sense in the New Testament that the death and resurrection of Jesus constituted a comprehensive victory over the powers of evil at work in the world. The result of this was twofold. First, that Jesus followers could be free from anything that could hold them back from living the sort of lives that please God and demonstrate the values of God's kingdom—free from excessive desire, addictions, and self-centeredness. And second, that the alternative reality of God's realm, based on love and peace, has been shown to be stronger than all the violence and rage of the world's despots, dictators, and empires. Paul shows in Romans 13 that the world's governments are subject to God, and in Philippians 2 he says that,

13. Wright, *Evil and the Justice of God*, 24.

14. Ibid., 43.

eventually, "every knee" will bow to the Lord Jesus, and includes in this every conceivable element in creation.

Christ's death and resurrection demonstrated the ultimate triumph of love over all the wickedness, violence, and hatred of human beings. Christ's death and vindication by God provides the pattern of life for Jesus followers, and their hope in the face of trial and oppression. Ultimately, Paul tells us towards the end of Romans 8 that nothing can separate us from God's love—and to a group of believers who were facing real hardship and danger as they sought to live under the Lordship of Christ in the heart of the kingdom of Caesar, he includes being persecuted, going hungry or becoming destitute, and being threatened with death. Jesus followers through the centuries who have found their lives wracked with difficulty or oppression because of their faith have understood the reality of these words. Joni Eareckson Tada, who became a quadriplegic in an accident as a girl, was able, remarkably, to say after forty years of suffering in her wheelchair, "The flow of wise, loving, concerned, attentive, watchful, impassioned, infinitely caring thoughts [of God] surge on and on, all day, all night, for as long as you live."[15]

Through living out the alternative reality of Jesus's Lordship in a here-and-now community, we can see how groups of Jesus followers from the earliest days to the present have found it possible to cope with poverty and oppression through their commitment to love and support for one another. This is the lived-out expression of Jesus's kingdom and demonstrates that there is a different kind of life possible, based on mutual love, forgiveness, and justice, which challenges the surrounding self-seeking culture where violence or the threat of violence is usually a key component. Sadly, of course, there are plenty of examples in church history where the Christian church has aligned itself to the dominant power of its day, and has exchanged love for oppression, meekness for power, and dependence on God for wealth.

Notwithstanding this, though, the power of love can, and does, bring about real change. This can be seen both at a personal level and at the level of widespread change in a society. A good recent example of this is the young woman who courageously talked down a school gunman. The gunman, dressed in black and armed with an AK-47 and other weapons, had burst into a suburban Atlanta elementary school. "He had a look on him that he was willing to kill," Antoinette Tuff recalled. How often have these

15. Eareckson Tada, *A Place of Healing*, 102.

situations turned horribly wrong? But in the face of terror, Antoinette Tuff used kindness and love to dissipate a potential nightmare. After the police had arrived and had started firing at the gunman, Tuff reasoned with him. She can be heard saying during a call to a news station, which the gunman had requested, "It's going to be all right, sweetie. I just want you to know I love you, though, OK? And I'm proud of you. That's a good thing that you're just giving up and don't worry about it. We all go through something in life. No, you don't want that. You going to be OK."[16]

But not only is love and compassion a powerful weapon at a personal level, it can work at a macro level in society too. Desmond Tutu, who as an archbishop saw his people suffer under the injustice of apartheid in South Africa, but who also saw the end of that oppressive system, once said, "Do your little bit of good where you are; it's those little bits of good put together that overwhelm the world." In the midst of brutality and oppression, Tutu believed that human beings were part of the same family and were made for togetherness, goodness, and for compassion, and saw that dream become a reality. His conviction, born out of his Christian faith, was that human beings were made for loving. "If we don't love," he said, "we will be like plants without water."[17]

South Africa emerged out of the nightmare of apartheid, certainly not unscathed, but without the bloodbath that many people, including Tutu, had feared. Part of this was due to the strong leadership shown by Nelson Mandela and Tutu himself. Mandela said that, as he walked out the door of the prison toward the gate that would lead to his freedom after twenty-seven years of incarceration, "I knew if I didn't leave my bitterness and hatred behind, I'd still be in prison."[18]

Remarkably, after all those years in prison, and the naked aggression of the apartheid system which had so terribly scarred the black population, Mandela somehow found a way to forgive his tormentors, even inviting one of his white jailers to attend, as an honored guest, his inauguration as president.

But not only did Mandela adopt an attitude of forgiveness and compassion for himself, these were the values that he championed as South Africa made the transition to a working democracy, with a constitution which

---

16. Tuff, interviews with ABC News and *Forbes*.

17. Quotes drawn from Desmond Tutu Peace Foundation and Tutu Foundation UK Facebook post.

18. Clinton, *Living History*, 236.

protected the rights of all South Africans. At the same time, he understood that the past must not be forgotten, and he helped form the country's Truth and Reconciliation Commission, which spent two years investigating crimes committed both by apartheid supporters and by its opponents.

"To be free," Mr. Mandela once said, "is not merely to cast off one's chains, but to live in a way that respects and enhances the freedom of others."[19] Mandela understood that forgiveness is underpinned by a compassion that recognizes the humanity we share—even when some of us engage in monstrous behavior—for which we must take moral responsibility.

After Nelson Mandela passed away at the end of 2013, Bill Clinton was reported saying that Mandela would be remembered as a man of "uncommon grace and compassion, for whom abandoning bitterness and embracing adversaries was not just a political strategy but a way of life."[20]

Sojourner Truth was born in 1797 into slavery in Ulster County, New York. She had a succession of owners, one of whom was particularly cruel and who beat her every day. She fell in love with a slave from another farm, Robert, but Robert's owner opposed the marriage and savagely beat him to the point where he died from his injuries. Sojourner managed to escape to freedom in 1826, and was taken in by Isaac and Maria Van Wagenen. Here she had a profound religious experience, of which she said, "God revealed Himself to me with all of the suddenness of lightning."[21] Later in her life, she explained, "I was civilized not by people, but by Jesus. When I got religion, I found some work to do to benefit somebody."[22]

Before her conversion, her terrible experiences as a slave had led her to urge God to kill "all the white people and not leave enough for seed." But after her encounter with Jesus Christ, she said, "Yeah God, I love everyone and the white people, too."[23] Truth said that others told her "There's the white folks that have abused you, and beat you, and abused your people— think of them." Her response to this was "then there came another rush of love through my soul, and I cried out loud—'Lord, Lord, I can love even the white folks!'"[24]

19. Mandela, *Long Walk to Freedom*, 624.

20. Clinton, "on the Passing of Nelson Mandela."

21. Whalin, *Sojourner Truth*, Kindle location 586–87.

22. Ibid., Kindle location 596–97.

23. Ibid., Kindle location 597–99.

24. Ibid., Kindle location 1676–77.

Sojourner began her work as an abolitionist, speaking out fearlessly about the evils of slavery. In due course, her campaigning included women's rights, prison reform, and opposition to capital punishment. She became such a well-known proponent of freedom that President Lincoln, whom she met, told her that he had known of her work for a long time, even before he had become president.

The Liberator, an abolitionist newspaper of the time, said of Truth, "But the truly Christian spirit [that] pervades all she says endears her to all who know her. Though she has suffered all the ills of slavery, she forgives all who have wronged her most freely. She said her home should be open to the man who had held her as a slave and who had so much wronged her. She would feed him and take care of him if he was hungry and poor. 'Oh friends,' she said, 'pity the poor slaveholder, and pray for him. It troubles me more than anything else, what will become of the poor slaveholder, in all his guilt and all his impenitence.'"[25]

Sojourner Truth was motivated by both an urgent desire to see justice and by the love of God. She acted courageously for equal rights, risking humiliation and her own personal safety, but her fearless expression of God's truth, justice, and love played a major part in the battles against slavery, racism, and discrimination against both African Americans and women.

Northern Ireland, my own country, is also a remarkable example of the power of love and compassion to overcome evil. In 1988, the violence of "the Troubles" had escalated to an unbearable level and many felt it was getting out of control. With the murder of two British servicemen who had inadvertently found themselves in the vicinity of a Provisional IRA funeral, it was a powder keg situation. Father Alec Reid, a Redemptorist priest, was on the scene and tried to protect the two British soldiers from being shot by the IRA by lying on the ground between them. Unfortunately, the two soldiers were shot and killed in cold blood, after Reid was heaved away by the gunmen, one of whom told him, "Get up, or I'll shoot you as well." Father Reid tried to save the soldiers by giving them mouth-to-mouth resuscitation and when he realized he could do nothing more, he gave them the last rites.

During this incident, Father Reid had a letter in his pocket, one of a series of messages from republicans to the nationalist politician John Hume, which are credited with being the catalyst for bringing about the eventual IRA cease-fire. The efforts of this brave Christian, along with

25. Ibid., Kindle location 1461–63.

others who joined his peacemaking efforts from other denominations, including the Presbyterians and Methodists, pulled Northern Ireland back from the brink and played a vital role in the peace process which ensued. The courage, faith, and love of these people proved, in the end, to make the difference in a way that violence and counterviolence never had, or could.

At both a personal level and the level of society, time and time again—when given the chance—love and forgiveness prove themselves more powerful than the powers of wickedness. It is the contention in the New Testament that Jesus, in his death and resurrection, has overcome the power of evil—and when Jesus followers believe in that victory and courageously live out the values of the kingdom of God, including love, forgiveness, and justice, real change can come about.

So What About the Devil?

Aside from the account of Jesus's temptations in the synoptic Gospels, the devil or Satan is mentioned some sixty-two times in the New Testament. So, while the devil clearly does not seem to be featured very prominently, there is enough mention to convince us that the New Testament writers took the idea seriously. Satan, whose name means "adversary," is clearly seen as the embodiment of everything that is evil, everything that opposes God, God's people, and God's justice.

The devil is the one who tempts Jesus to alter his means of being the Messiah; who inspires the betrayer, Judas Iscariot; who holds human beings in darkness (Acts 26:18); who opposes Jesus followers (1 Cor 7:5; 1 Thess 2:18); who has the power of death (Heb 2:14); and who will be defeated at the last by God (Rev 20:10).

In the twenty-first century, it is, perhaps, hard for us to know what to make of this whole idea—for many people, believing in God is a big enough challenge without having to believe in a personal devil. And yet, the New Testament not only talks about the devil as the enemy, but makes references to a whole cosmology of "principalities, powers and demons," which seem to be hold human beings in thrall.

Walter Wink, who has written on this area extensively and very helpfully, notes the following:

> If Satan has any reality at all, it is . . . as a profound experience of
> numinous, uncanny power in the psychic and historic lives of real
> people. Satan is the real interiority of a society that idolatrously
> pursues its own enhancement as the highest good. Satan is the

spirituality of an epoch, the peculiar constellation of alienation, greed, inhumanity, oppression, and entropy that characterizes a specific period of history as a consequence of human decisions to tolerate and even further such a state of affairs.[26]

For Wink, it is unimportant whether Satan is a metaphysical reality or not. What matters is the experiential reality of evil, which is "far more pervasive in human experience than most people are aware."[27] C. S. Lewis notes the danger of ignoring the reality of evil in the preface to his *Screwtape Letters*—"There are two equal and opposite errors into which our race can fall about the devils. One is to disbelieve in their existence. The other is to believe, and to feel an excessive and unhealthy interest in them."[28]

Satan is a life-quenching power which desires murder ("the devil is a murderer from the beginning," John 8:44), a slanderer or false accuser, and the "father of lies" (John 8:44), who opposes the truth of God's inexhaustible love for us. On a personal level, we are faced with Satan's lies about our worth as human beings, when, on the one hand, if you're one of the majority of people in the world who live in poverty, that very physical and economic poverty creates a poverty of spirit that keeps people from believing that their lives could or should be any different than the one which is blighted by lack. And on the other hand, if you live in a wealthy Western society, your self-worth is attacked by the advertising industry, which needs you to believe you need ever more—and the latest!—products to have a fulfilled happy life, and by a pervasive media that promotes appearances, fashions, and lifestyles as necessary to human worth. These death-dealing lies lead to a range of desperate results from deep unhappiness, to mental illness, to abusive behavior, to addictions, to suicide. God's truth, on the other hand, speaks of the inestimable worth of every human being. Humans were made in God's image, meant to be God's stewards and fellow workers within the world, and are loved and cherished by God. The New Testament is full of assertions of God's love for us—"See what great love the Father has lavished on us, that we should be called children of God," says the author of 1 John— and it is this truth that gives meaning, value, and purpose to our lives.[29]

26. Wink, *Unmasking the Powers*, 2.

27. Ibid.

28. Lewis, *The Screwtape Letters*, ix.

29. For a detailed argument regarding the basis of human worth, which concludes "that if God loves a human being . . . that love bestows great worth on that human being," see Wolterstorff, *Justice*, 360.

At a macrosocietal level, the devil's lies include all sense that one group of human beings—the one to which *I* belong—is superior to another, whether on the basis of race, gender, nationality, intelligence, or "our (superior) way of life." Such are the foundations of conflict, oppression, violence, and war. In Acts 13, we have the story of Barnabas and Paul's encounter with the Roman proconsul in Cyprus, whose sagely consultant, the prophet Bar-Jesus, tries to divert him from his interest in the apostles' message. Paul strikes Bar-Jesus with blindness, telling him that he is a "son of the devil," and is an "enemy of all justice." By trying to stop the Roman official from embracing the good news of Jesus the Messiah, Bar-Jesus was stopping the gospel of peace from reaching the local corridors of power and thus keeping the status quo in terms of Roman injustice, at least in the life of this one official and his domain. The story highlights for us another hugely important way in which Satan works—to oppose justice. The injustice perpetrated by human beings on other human beings for the cause of economic gain, a sense of racial superiority, for the sheer love of dominating, or for any other reason is, quite simply, a primary work of the devil.

There is more afoot here than simply the harm done by individual human beings. As Wink says, when society "idolatrously pursues its own enhancement as the highest good," there is, so to speak, a foothold given to the devil and, in so much as we collude with the forces of greed, inhumanity, and oppression, we reinforce the negative powers at work in the world and the potential to be caught in their nexus. The spirit of the age is more than simply a way of characterizing the nature of a particular culture—"the satanic is . . . crystallized in the institutional values and arrangements in which we find ourselves."[30] We can think of circumstances in recent history where there seem to be great powers at work in societies or groups of people, driving them on to great evil, which appear to be greater than any one individual—one has only to think of Nazi Germany, or the Bosnian or Rwandan genocides in the 1990s, or indeed, the treatment of Southern blacks in the USA during the Jim Crow years to appreciate the cumulative power of evil.

The New Testament language of the devil and of the "powers," then, although written in a prescientific age where the language of the numinous was widely used to describe phenomena that people could not explain, points to real, negative forces at work in the world, which we would do well to recognize and, with God's help, resist. Wink talks of "the social

30. Wink, *Unmasking the Powers*, 31.

sedimentation of human choices for evil," which can manifest itself is a variety of ways "in person and in society."[31]

Against whatever dark forces we may experience within or without, the gospel of Jesus Christ stands as a bright light able to dispel all the darkness. "The reason the Son of God appeared was to destroy the works of the devil" (1 John 3:8). The New Testament writers were convinced that Christ had won a decisive victory over evil, meaning three things—that Jesus followers could live free personally from the influence of any dark powers at work in the world; that Jesus followers could model a new kind of communal life where love and forgiveness prevailed over greed, violence, and selfishness; and that, in the end, the devil, as the personification of all evil, will end up being consigned to the "lake of fire" (Rev 20:10). God will have the last word and evil will, in the end, be banished from God's world.

The Devil Don't Have No Music

As we have seen, the blues have had an association with the devil over the years. Lonnie Johnson, often thought of as the original single-note blues guitar soloist, recorded "Devil's Got the Blues" in 1938, where he equates the blues with the devil—"Blues'll leave your heart full of trouble and your po' mind full of hell" is followed by "Blues and the devil is your two closest friends."

There has been, however, a steady stream of blues songs that have celebrated the defeat of the devil, the fact of the Lord's power being stronger than the devil's, and the need, as the author of James says, to "resist the devil" (Jas 4:7). Rev. Gary Davis, in "Say No to the Devil," recorded in 1961, advises, "Well the devil is a deceiver, Say no to the devil, he won't treat nobody right. Well the devil is a big liar, say no."

The same theme of the lies of the devil to which the New Testament attests is taken up by Otis Taylor in his 2012 album *Contraband*. In the opening song, "Devil's Gonna Lie," we get two lines repeated over and over—"The devil's gonna lie, When he needs to," sung over a two-chord blues riff. For Taylor, one senses the devil isn't so much a person as the personification of evil at work in the world through systems and institutions that abuse and exploit. And lies are always the tools of such evil. As the Apostle John said, the devil is a liar and the father of lies. The song starts off with the foreboding sounds of a cornet and discordant electric guitar,

31. Ibid., 25.

with moaning and manic laughter. It's the devil all right. But before long we get a gospel choir joining in and by the end with the full sound of the band, the choir and Otis seem to hit a note of triumph. The lies of the devil don't get the last word.

We considered in the previous section how our complicity with evil both adds to the force of evil and to our own entanglement and ensnarement. A number of blues songs seem to recognize this, and urge us to resist the pull. Bo Carter's 1938 "Go Back Old Devil" tells the "old devil" to "get back on your shelf," while bang up to date, Chicago blues artist Lurrie Bell's song "Don't Let the Devil Ride" from his 2012 album *The Devil Don't Have No Music* captures the danger well: "Don't let the devil ride, 'cause if you let him ride, he'll want to drive."

One of the most original, current blues bands, the North Mississippi Allstars, are also alert to this danger—"If you raise the devil, you can't keep the devil down," they sing in "Keep the Devil Down" from their 2009 album *Hernando.*

The Reverend Payton's Big Damn Band in "Devils Look Like Angels" (*Between the Ditches,* 2012) reminds us that the "Devil don't live down in hell, devil lives here and he's doing very well." This sense of the immediacy of evil is referred to in the story of Cain and Abel in Genesis 4. Cain gets gripped by anger at his brother, and prior to his murderous action, God tells him that "sin is crouching at the door. Its desire is for you, but you must rule over it." In addition to the thrall of institutionalized evil, each one of us is at the mercy of our own inner compulsions and desires, many of which result in relationship problems, of which murder is the extreme example.

One result of our own personal failures to deal with what "crouches at the door" is unfaithfulness. Howlin' Wolf captures the true nature of this in his song simply entitled "Evil." Wolf makes us imagine a partner a long way from home while his lover is being unfaithful. "Evil is goin' on wrong, I am warnin' ya brother, You better watch your happy home."

While it is incumbent upon us to resist the devil's lies, to rule over our inner compulsions and to oppose the forces of dehumanization within our societies, in whatever form they assail us—ultimately the gospel's triumphant message is that evil will not, in the end, have the last word, because of the death, resurrection, and exaltation of Jesus. Irish bluesman Brian Houston hits this positive note in "Devil Gonna Run," from his 2013 release *Mercy.* Because, "Jesus rose up from the grave," the "devil gonna run, run from the man of God" (and presumably, the woman of God!).

In the end, despite all the talk of the blues and the devil, as Lurrie Bell reminds us, "the devil ain't got no music." Far from this or that form of music belonging to the devil, "the devil ain't got no music, that's why his home is hell . . . Satan has got no song." In the end, song belongs to the Lord; music is too good a thing for the devil to own. And in the end, evil will not triumph—the risen Christ is Lord and "he must reign until he has put all his enemies under his feet" (1 Cor 15:25).

Listening Guide

Eric Clapton, *Me and Mr. Johnson,* Reprise, 2004

Son House, *The Original Delta Blues*, Sony, 1998

Lonnie Johnson, *All Time Blues Greats,* Stardust, 2008

Lurrie Bell, *The Devil Don't Have No Music,* Aria B. G. Records, 2012

The Reverend Peyton's Big Damn Band, *Between The Ditches,* SideOneDummy Records, 2012

nine

Worried Minds

Beating the Blues

Therefore I tell you, do not be anxious about your life, what you will eat
or what you will drink, nor about your body, what you will put on. Is
not life more than food, and the body more than clothing? Look at the
birds of the air: they neither sow nor reap nor gather into barns, and
yet your heavenly Father feeds them. Are you not of more value than
they? And which of you by being anxious can add a single hour to his
span of life? And why are you anxious about clothing? Consider the
lilies of the field, how they grow: they neither toil nor spin, yet I tell you,
even Solomon in all his glory was not arrayed like one of these. But if
God so clothes the grass of the field, which today is alive and tomorrow
is thrown into the oven, will he not much more clothe you, O you of
little faith? Therefore do not be anxious, saying, "What shall we eat?" or
"What shall we drink?" or "What shall we wear?" For the Gentiles seek
after all these things, and your heavenly Father knows that you need
them all. But seek first the kingdom of God and his righteousness, and
all these things will be added to you. Therefore do not be anxious about
tomorrow, for tomorrow will be anxious for itself. Sufficient for the day
is its own trouble.

MATTHEW 6:25–34

To Be Poor Is to Be Anxious

As we have seen, in the Sermon, Jesus is explaining to his followers what life is like for those who welcome the rule or kingdom of God. God's reign runs on entirely different principles than any kingdom or government we're used to. It's a kingdom of peace and peacemakers. It's a kingdom based on justice; it's a kingdom based on love for others, including enemies; it's a kingdom where the poor and those who lament for the injustice in the world are blessed; it's a kingdom where gentleness holds sway. It's so different from the way that the world works that Jesus followers are likely to be insulted and persecuted, so that the way of love involves deep personal sacrifice and clear-eyed devotion to God trumps all other allegiances.

Things are so different in this conception of the world, and the present danger to those who will give themselves to it so great, that Jesus deems it necessary to deal with the problem of anxiety. Living in a countercultural way, Jesus realized, is no picnic, and his followers needed to realize that, despite the sacrifice and the insults and persecution to be suffered, they could trust God to provide for them. Their "heavenly Father" was utterly faithful and could be relied upon, even for the basics of life. "Don't be anxious," said Jesus. His followers simply had to live in a way that is commensurate with God's kingdom, in a way that demonstrates God's kingdom, and God would provide. God "knows that you need all these things." So don't worry, all that you need will be "added to you." On this basis there is no point in worrying about tomorrow—that's just too much worry to have to carry. Each day has enough worry on its own.

To the largely impoverished people of Palestine and the Roman Mediterranean world who became followers of Jesus in the early centuries of Christianity—and, indeed, to a great many people in today's world who suffer from the effects of war, hunger, and deprivation—Jesus's words are vital. For the world's poor, anxiety is an integral part of life. Today, the daily experience of millions of people is anxiety about whether they can earn enough money to feed and clothe themselves and their families, or anxiety about their security—whether today might be the day when the militia arrives and violence is visited upon them—or anxiety about whether they can continue to afford their children's education. To be poor is to have your life choices dramatically reduced; to be poor is to be anxious.

As we have seen, however, the earliest followers of Jesus took his preaching about the rule of God seriously and built little communities that resisted the rule of the world and sought to live out God's new world that Jesus had come to bring. As they cared for each other, loved one another, and let that compassion ooze out into the wider world, they discovered that it really was possible to leave the normal anxiety of life behind and put their trust in God. In these small, countercultural communities, faith and trust replaced worry and anxiety.

Consider the Apostle Paul, writing to the Jesus followers in Philippi in the middle of the first century. At the time, he himself was languishing in a Roman jail, in chains and completely uncertain of his future, whether he would be taken and beheaded, or would live to be able to come and visit his sisters and brothers in Philippi again. Incredibly, he tells the Philippians about his "joy," and suggests that even were he to die, it would be a "gain" for him.

The letter is awash with joy, and Paul tells his fellow believers that they too are to "rejoice always." Given the situation of the Philippians—"suffering" and "experiencing conflict" (Phil 1:29–30)—this might sound rather trite, if Paul's own dire situation in prison were not at least as difficult as that of the Philippians. As a group of relatively poor people in the Roman colony of Philippi, the Christians there were likely suffering economic hardship directly arising from their decision to follow this illicit and suspicious Jewish sect.[1] It is in this context, then, that Paul writes about the experience of joy.

The Philippians had experienced the tough reality of which Jesus had warned in the Sermon—of being persecuted and insulted for the sake of the justice of God's kingdom—and Paul, like Jesus, advocates a radical trust in God as the antidote to the anxiety that their difficult circumstances engendered. "Don't be anxious about anything," Paul says towards the end of his letter—rather bring your needs and requests to God. Oh—and be thankful too, he suggests! (Phil 4:4ff.). What's more, despite the harsh treatment they had been receiving from their neighbors, the Philippians were to continue to live out the Jesus-kingdom value of gentleness. They were to let their "gentleness show in [their] treatment of everyone," here directly echoing the meekness, mercy showing and peacemaking of the Sermon's Beatitudes and Jesus's love instructions at the end of Matthew 5.

If the Philippians could continue their radical life of mutual and overflowing love, could put their trust so fully in God, despite their difficulties, that they would be able to rejoice and give thanks, then Paul told them that

---

1. This is explained in some detail in Oakes, *Philippians.*

"the peace of God that exceeds all understanding will keep your hearts and minds safe in Christ Jesus" (Phil 4:1).

Here we see how, in extreme circumstances, early followers of Jesus were able to put into practice his teaching about not being anxious, but rather to trust God, no matter what, Because Paul and these early believers were convinced that a new world had broken into the present one, that there truly was a new creation of which they were a part, and that "the sufferings of this present time are not worthy to be compared with the glory that is to be revealed to us" (Rom 8:18). Their communal life together, enlivened by the Spirit, convinced them that it was possible to live out the kingly rule of God, with all the difficulties that that might bring, through having a deep-seated trust in the goodness and faithfulness of God.

Worried Life Blues

We've seen already how the uncertainties and trials of life for black people living in the Southern states under Jim Crow left them with a "worried mind." Tampa Red, in 1931, in "Depression Blues," sang,

> If I could tell my troubles, it would give my poor heart ease
> But depression has got me, somebody help me please.

Anxiety was an integral part of life—black people were worried about having enough money to make ends meet, about losing a job, about the future of their children, and about the dangers of interaction with white people. Blind Blake complained in "No Dough Blues" in 1928, "As it's a hard time, good man can't get no dough."

They were, however, also worried about much more sinister threats. We have already considered the very real possibility that existed for black men in particular of being lynched for some petty, perceived wrongdoing, or simply for being black. They were also worried about the possibility of falling foul of the law and ending up as caught in a new, pernicious form of slavery in the iniquitous system of peonage that was part of the economic life of Southern states from the period after the Civil War until 1945.

Douglas Blackmon's shocking and heartrending book, *Slavery By Another Name*, chronicles the way in which hundreds of thousands of black Americans were reenslaved during this period. Blackmon charts in considerable detail the way in which local law enforcement, the judiciary, and local businesses conspired to arrest black men on trumped up or minor charges, convict them in court, and then lease them to mining and timber companies or farms, where they were often worked to death. Conditions for these "neoslaves" were even worse that it had been for their forebears in antebellum times, in that at least slave owners before the war felt they had some vested interest in the health of the slave and so moderated their treatment to some degree. In this new form of slavery, company owners and personnel felt no such responsibility—if a black man died in the course of his work, nobody asked why and there would always be another "convict" to take his place. Consequently these new slaves were kept in the most atrocious conditions, fed badly, and worked as much as they possibly could be, and more.[2]

At the Sloss-Sheffield mines in Coalburg, Alabama, where several hundred prisoners had been purchased from judges and sheriffs, a state inspector was appalled at the conditions in which the men worked and lived—he called it "disastrous," and another visitor called the death rate there, which ran at 34 percent, "enormous" and "frightful." A special committee that studied the convict system in the state in 1889 said that many of the black miners had "not seen the sun in months." The men were beaten regularly and if they tried to escape were either killed or flogged mercilessly.[3]

As well as these appalling conditions, Blackmon notes the nature of the "crimes" of which these men had been convicted in the first place—bigamy, homosexuality, "miscegenation," illegal voting, "false pretense" (breaking newly enacted laws that were designed to prevent black men from leaving a farming job before the end of a crop season), using obscene language, gambling, selling cotton after the sun set. Nothing, in other words, which remotely deserved imprisonment, never mind the brutalization into which the men were sold.

The fact of the matter is that these charges were an excuse to enslave black men. The system was widespread and it lasted well into the twentieth century, until the end of World War II.

Local sheriffs and court officials found that they could earn a great deal more than their salaries by playing an active role in the new slavery. Black men were charged fees for their arrest, court appearances, and transportation to the company that leased them. The company would then pay these "debts" on behalf of a prisoner, who then had to work, often much longer than his sentence, in order to pay off the debt.

---

2. Blackmon, *Slavery by Another Name*.

3. Ibid., 98–99.

The leasing system was widespread. Not only were the mining and lumber industries active in utilizing black slave labor, but "thousands of white land owners and local businesses in the countryside and provincial towns" took advantage of the opportunity of labor that cost virtually nothing. Typical of white attitudes was that expressed by James Tomas Helfin, US Senator for Alabama in 1901: "I believe . . . that God Almighty intended the negro to be the servant of the white man." That being the case, the convict leasing system was entirely justified, and could be implemented by whatever brutal means were required—"everybody knows the character of a Negro," said an Alabama official around the same time, "and knows that there is no punishment in the world that can take the place of the lash with him. He must be controlled in this way."[4]

Blackmon gives an example of the danger which beset black men in this period. In 1901, John Davis, a young man of twenty-three who owned a tiny farm near Nixburg, Alabama, went to visit his wife, who was very sick and who had gone to be looked after, at her parents' home in Goodwater, about twenty miles away. As he was making his way on foot after getting off the train, he was accosted by a white constable who asked him for money. Davis's refusal led to him being arrested on the pretext of him owing the constable money. A makeshift court the next day found Davis guilty and he was taken to meet John Pace, who owned a large farm nearby. Pace paid Davis's "debt" and Davis was effectively sold into slavery on Pace's farm, having been made to sign a document that he could not have read, which bound him to "work . . . until I have paid . . . in full," to be "locked up in the cell at night," and to submit to "such treatment as other convicts." John Davis, a hardworking, poor, black farmer, had been ensnared in a slavery ring which routinely delivered innocent black men into captivity on the Pace farm.[5]

This seizure of black men was now happening all across the South, with innocent black men being made "convicts" and ending up as slave labor in sawmills, mines, and quarries, where they were treated abominably and from where many never returned. This system of neoslavery persisted across the South for around eighty years—in 1930, shockingly, Blackmon notes that "Roughly half of all African Americans—or 4.8 million—lived in the Black Belt region of the South . . . the great majority of whom were almost certainly trapped in some form of coerced labor."

4. Ibid., 122.
5. Ibid., 117ff.

There had been a grand jury investigation of "peonage" in the South that led to a series of trials of some of the new slave owners in 1903, but these failed to deal with the issue and the peonage system was effectively ratified and continued free from legal interference until World War II. It was only in 1941, when the US entered World War II and a confrontation with fascism brought home the problem of the lack of democracy and oppression that existed in the Southern states for its black population, that the US took definite steps to end "peonage" or neoslavery. US Attorney General Francis Biddle issued a directive "acknowledging the long history of the unwritten federal law enforcement policy to ignore most reports of involuntary servitude."[6] The Justice Department began to vigorously prosecute companies that coerced black people into peonage, and by the early 1950s the reports of involuntary servitude had become just a trickle. Seventy-four years of the most brutal neoslavery came to an end.

It is no accident, then, that a great body of blues songs originated from the experience of black men in custody.

The movement to end convict leasing in Mississippi resulted in the creation of Parchman Farm, and the man behind it was Governor James K. Vardaman, who had used racism and fears of black lawlessness to gain power. Vardaman believed that the end of slavery had eroded "proper discipline, strong work habits, and respect for white authority" in young black men, and that a prison farm—effectively an efficient slave plantation—was required. Parchman Farm was set on 20,000 acres in the Mississippi Delta region, and was organized as slave plantations had been before the Civil War, complete with "sergeants" (overseers), "trustees" (slave drivers), and "gunmen" (the convicts who toiled under the gun of a trustee). Effectively these convicts—of whom many were imprisoned for trivial offenses—toiled for the state of Mississippi, earning it large profits, and creating an ongoing incentive for the state to arrest and imprison African Americans.

There have been a number of blues songs written about Parchman Farm and several blues musicians were imprisoned there, including Bukka White and Son House. In 1939, folklorist Alan Lomax recorded White and others at the farm for the Library of Congress.

White's song "Parchman Blues," as we have already seen, draws attention to the nature of the work in Parchman—from the "dawn of day" to the "settin' of the sun." The prison's brutality was the stuff of legend. One of the few ways to be released early was for one prisoner to kill another that was

6. Ibid., 377.

thought to be trying to escape and be rewarded for this. State farms like Parchman and prison chain gangs kept both those who were guilty of violent crimes and those guilty of simply violating the racist Jim Crow system in inhuman conditions. A great many blues musicians recorded songs that give us a record of Southern prisons in the 1920s and 1930s.

Mose Allison, American jazz/blues pianist and singer, born in 1927, gives us a good insight in his "Parchman Farm Blues."

> Well I'm sittin' over here on Parchman Farm
> . . . And I ain't never done no man no harm
> Well I'm puttin' that cotton in an eleven-foot sack
> . . . With a twelve gauge shotgun at my back.

Furry Lewis, from Memphis, sang about the inevitability of ending up in the penitentiary once he ended up in the court of "Judge Harsh." He sings about heading to prison despite never having harmed a man. Sadly the judge won't be bribed, and the penitentiary looms:

> They arrest me for murder, I ain't never harmed a man
> Women hollered murder and I ain't raised my hand . . .
> Because I'm arrested baby, please don't grieve and moan
> Penitentiary seems just like my home
> People all hollering about what in the world they will do
> Lots of people had justice and been in penitentiary too.

One of the remarkable prison songs recorded by Alan Lomas was a harmonica-voice duet from Alex and Tangle Eye. In "Prison Blues," Tangle Eye sings hauntingly:

> Well now y'all be standing around the courthouse babe
> Lord knows when Judge Davis give me my time
> . . . When I begin to leave my baby crying
> Lord knows Mr. Judge you give him too long
> Said now that's all right baby
> Lord knows I'll make it over one old day
> Said now that's all right baby
> I'll make it over one old day.

> Now some of the days soon, I'll make it back home
> Now fare you well, fare you well babe
> Lord knows I'm on my last go-round
> Now fare you well, fare you well
> Lord knows I'm on my last go-round
> Well you know if I can live to be in this town.

> Babe I won't be hollering
> Down in prison no more.

So prevalent was the penitentiary in the life the black communities, blues singers who didn't themselves experience its harsh reality had prison songs in their repertoire. Blind Lemon Jefferson recorded "Prison Cell Blues" in 1928:

> Got a red-eyed captain and a squabbling boss
> Got a mad dog sergeant
> honey and he won't knock off
> I asked the government to knock some days off my time
> Well the way I'm treated, I'm about to lose my mind
> I wrote to the governor, please turn me a loose
> Since I didn't get no answer I know it ain't no use.

The common complaints of the prisoner were about loneliness, the severity of the work regime, and difficulties with the captain, boss, and sergeant, all covered in Jefferson's song. He also mentions writing to the governor, which was often done often, though rarely doing any good.

Hard labor is a recurring theme in these prison blues and could refer to working on farms, building levees, or working in mines. Peg Leg Howell in 1929 recorded "Ball and Chain Blues," about being part of a chain gang working in a mine. There was scarcely a worse fate for a man:

> I asked the judge what might be my fine
> Get a pick and shovel, dig down in the mine
> I told the judge, I ain't been here before
> If you give me light sentence, I won't come here no more.
>
> Mr. Judge Mr. Judge, please don't break so hard
> I always been a poor boy, never hurt no John
> So the next day they carried the poor boy away
> Said the next day I had a ball and chain
> Take the stripes off my back, chains from around my legs
> This ball and chain about to kill me dead.

And long sentences were often meted out, far in excess of the crime or infraction of the law. This song from Cannon's Jug Stompers, "Viola Lee Blues," from 1928, captures this injustice:

> The judge he pleaded, clerk he wrote it down,
> Clerk he wrote it down, indeedy . . .

Some got six months . . . some got one solid year, indeedy . . .
But me and my buddy, got lifetime here.

The system of life in the South served to impoverish its black population, causing all the uncertainties and worries that poverty brings. On top of the lack of choice that marked all of life and all the anxieties that poverty brought, African Americans in the Deep South faced real fears about a system of "law" that was rigorously enforced and was used to keep them "in their place" and, shockingly, was used widely to entrap them back into slavery. Worried minds, anxious minds, this was normal life for African Americans at this time.

So it is for the poor and oppressed everywhere, like the poor people to whom Jesus spoke in Galilee, "Don't be anxious. Your Father knows about your situation."

An Age of Anxiety

The poor, then, have good reason to be anxious. The crazy thing is that those of us who are relatively wealthy—basically the vast majority of people who live in the developed world—somehow conspire to have our own anxious minds. We who are clothed, housed, warm (or cool, depending on where you live), educated, healthy, able to work, entertained day and night—we, too, somehow are anxious, have worried minds. How can this be?

About 18 percent of adults in the United States suffer from anxiety disorders, which are the most common mental illness in the country, according to the Anxiety and Depression Society of America.[7] These include panic attacks, phobias, obsessive compulsive disorder, and generalized anxiety.

People are worrying about big, small, real, and imaginary problems. And as a result they often find themselves with a constant feeling of stress and tension. But it's not just those with anxiety disorders who suffer from a worried mind.

Walter Brueggemann suggests that "anxiety of an acute kind is . . . peculiarly poignant in our society just now and . . . it constitutes the central

7. www.adaa.org/about-adaa/press-room/facts-statistics. In the UK, anxiety disorders affect around 9 percent of the population—www.mentalhealth.org.uk/help-information/mental-health-statistics/.

social reality to which we seek to make [a] pastoral response."[8] The pursuit of money, control, and power that dominates our political discourse, economic system, and daily life contrives to create a restless anxiety which results in exploitative practices and disturbs our peace. No matter where we sit in the consumption-based economic system in which we live, we are, as a matter of course, caught in its anxious, unceasing, and exhausting wake.

Brueggemann shines a light on the reality of our modern world with studies of the stories of the Israelites in Egypt and the Israelite king, Solomon. In a brilliant analysis of the exodus story, Brueggemann characterizes the Egyptian system under Pharaoh as one of "production and consumption," with its major output being "systemic anxiety that pervaded every level of society." He explains how Pharaoh's ambitious state-building program, which involved the Israelite slaves as brickmakers, caught up both Pharaoh and slaves in a deep, unsatisfying anxiety about levels of production. "Why did you not finish the required quantity of bricks yesterday and today, as you did before?" the Israelite supervisors were asked, before being beaten (Exod 5:14). The dehumanizing Egyptian system comes down to the watchword, "Make more bricks."

"It is all about productivity at enormous human expense, without regard for human well-being."[9] Production and commoditization allied to an insatiable desire for political and economic power resulted in abusive, dehumanizing labor practices and a system shot through with anxiety for everyone involved in it.

Brueggemann finds a similar account of ruthless oppression resulting in a deadly anxiety in the biblical story of Solomon. This is particularly relevant, given the mention that Jesus makes of the king in the passage from the sermon that we are considering.

The presentation of Solomon in the 1 Kings narratives is one where a good king transforms a modest group of hill country people into a nation with region-wide prominence. As his name suggests, he was (supposedly) the bringer of shalom to his kingdom—freedom from enemies, prosperity, and well-being. "King Solomon excelled all the kings of the earth in riches and wisdom. The whole earth sought the presence of Solomon," reads 1 Kings 10:23–24.

For all the positive presentation of Solomon, though, there was another, more sinister aspect to his reign. As we read the biblical texts, we see

8. Brueggemann, *Disruptive Grace*, 55.

9. Ibid., 80.

how Solomon rises to power, vigorously competing with his brother Adonijah and eventually having him put to death, along with other senior figures in the royal court who were deemed to be a threat. His reign, celebrated by Israel's historians as a great success, was marked by the "exploitative rule and abusive economics that Israel had already experienced from Pharaoh long ago."[10]

Solomon married the daughter of Pharaoh and began, enthusiastically and for his own aggrandizement, an insatiable practice of accumulation, built on conscripted cheap labor (1 Kgs 5). The king's accumulation of breathtaking wealth seemed to know no bounds and included food (4:22–23), gold and ivory (10:14ff.), artistic works (4:32), women (700 princesses and 300 concubines, according to 11:3), and exotic animals (10:22).

Solomon's excesses were paid for by "forced labor" (5:14) and international arms trafficking (10:28–29 and 9:26–28). His temple was ultimately a display of his own dazzling wealth, much of it overlaid or made with gold (6:20–22 and 7:48–50)—it was the "epitome of the entire system of accumulation grounded in anxiety, aimed at monopoly, and accomplished by exploitation."[11]

Ultimately the verdict on Solomon's reign was a negative one—"the LORD was angry with Solomon, because his heart had turned away from the LORD . . . he did not obey what the LORD commanded" (11:9–10). This verdict is not as it might seem at first glance based solely on the king's religious allegiances—Solomon is indicted for not keeping the covenant and God's law (11:11), which precluded the sort of personal wealth and exploitation of the poor that characterized his reign. The result was to be the overthrow of his regime.

Many years later, after Solomon's great temple was destroyed, the prophet Jeremiah warned of the dangers of wisdom, might, and wealth—characteristics most clearly exhibited in Israel's history by Solomon, who had set in train the chain of events that eventually led to Jerusalem's downfall (Jer 9:23–24). Jeremiah contrasts these three characteristics to those of Yahweh—love, justice, and righteousness.

With this context, then, we can better consider the words of Jesus, who warns against anxiety about commodities—his disciples are not to worry about their lives, their food, what they have to drink, or their wardrobe! It's the pursuit of life's commodities that make us anxious and

10. Brueggemann, *Truth Speaks to Power*.
11. Ibid., 67.

restless—but, hey, says Jesus, look at the glories of God's creation, the birds and the flowers, which flourish and blossom, without the need for anxious accumulation. Contrast this, says Jesus, with the archetypal restless accumulator Solomon—"who, in all his glory, was not arrayed like one of these."

The anxiety of the wealthy—including both the seriously wealthy and the rest of us who are relatively wealthy—is in contrast with the worries of the poor. Our worries—much of the time—are not serious. Our entanglement with the world of accumulation and the defense of what we have ties us in to a negative spiral where we have much more than we need and yet somehow we never have enough.

There is always a new smartphone to upgrade to; there is always a new, more fashionable outfit to wear, a car to be replaced every two or three years, a new restaurant in town to sample, a new, bigger house to move to, a more exotic holiday this year than last year. We need to keep moving on—and up. That's progress, isn't it? That's capitalism at work, the best economic system the world has ever known. That's our *way of life*. So along we go, led by the insatiable need to grow the economy, and led by the need to defend it at all costs.

In UK airports, when you check the electronic board to see if your flight is boarding or not, you either get a gate number beside the flight or a message which says, "Relax and shop." The airports there are packed with shops and restaurants and there are very few seats for the weary traveler between flights to just sit and read or talk to a companion. The expectation is that you will fill your time with shopping. Relax and shop. Two words that actually are antithetical, but the propaganda all the time is "shop, acquire, possess and you'll be satisfied." So much so that the very action of shopping itself brings satisfaction and relaxation.

Except, of course, it rarely does. We need to stop for a moment; still the clamor of the advertising on our phones, iPads, laptops and TVs; take a break from the incessant flow of chatter, noise, and information on our social media and news channels—and let the words of Jesus calm that curious restlessness that somehow besets us no matter how much more we acquire. "Don't be anxious. Life is about more than consumption. Put your energy into seeking justice. And your heavenly father will look after you."

Trouble Will Soon Be Over

Blind Willie Johnson was born in 1897. Life was difficult enough for a poor black man at this time in Texas, but Willie's blindness contributed to a life of considerable hardship. As we have seen, his faith and his music enabled him to withstand the adversity of life, which was filled with worry. One of his standard songs was "Trouble Will Soon Be Over," which is a quite remarkable response to all that life had to throw at him. "God," he sings, "is my strong protection, he's my bosom friend"—despite the fact that "trouble arose all around me."

"Well, though my burden may be heavy, my enemies crush me down," expresses the reality of Willie Johnson's life. Yet this weight need not be too heavy, Willie asserts, because, "Christ is my burden bearer, he's my only friend." The result of this faith, defiant in the face of terrible odds, for Willie was twofold. First, "I'll take this yoke upon me and live a Christian life, take Jesus for my Savior, my burden will be light." And then, beyond this life, in the fullness of the kingdom to come, "Someday I'll rest with Jesus and wear a starry crown." And so, he sings confidently,

> Oh, trouble'll soon be over, sorrow will have an end
> Oh, trouble'll soon be over, sorrow will have an end.

Blind Willie Johnson, uneducated and poor, expresses eloquently the theological truth of the now and not yet of the anxiety-neutralizing kingdom of God. The reality of God's day has dawned in such a way that Willie could experience the presence of Christ in the midst of life's trials, as he sought to "live a Christian life." And there is coming a day when "sorrow will have an end," in which Willie and other faithful Jesus followers will share.

Don't Be Anxious

For those whose lives are blighted by poverty and oppression of one sort or another—like the black communities in the Southern states when the blues was growing up—worry and anxiety is an inevitable part of life. Anxiety, curiously, affects the wealthy as well, but here it is a restlessness that comes from having too much, from the psychological need to accumulate more. But, of course, in the end, all of us suffer from true anxiety from time to time. Worry that comes when we or someone we love contracts a serious or debilitating illness; worry over loss of a job and income, and how we're going to make ends meet; worry over teenage children making bad choices;

worry about things we've done in the past; worry about being able to please the new boss; worry about how we're going to make the payroll this month and pay the staff; worries about what people will think of us.

In situations like this it is the natural human response to worry. Some years ago I ran a small business and we came into a really tough period. My natural inclination was to double my efforts—if I could just work a bit harder, work longer hours, be more determined, we'd make it. I was driven by anxiety. I stumbled upon some words in Psalm 127:2 which are reflected in Jesus's teaching about worry in the Sermon: "It is vain for you to rise up early, to retire late, to eat the bread of painful labors; For He gives to His beloved even in his sleep." The words spoke directly to my anxious situation—getting up early, retiring late, and putting in long hours of painful labor were exactly what I was doing. I needed to realize that God was in control and that God was at work, even while I was sleeping and wasn't able to do anything about my situation. The situation remained difficult for some time, but I learned to release my anxiety to God and make some progress in trusting in God's grace.

Real worries, worries that have no real substance, worry that is part of the spirit of our grasping, accumulating age—worry assails us all at times, and Jesus's words in the Sermon powerfully address our worried minds: "Don't be anxious . . . your heavenly Father knows . . . seek first the kingdom of God and God's justice, and you will have everything you need."

Finally, we must note that the peaceful, anxiety-free life for Jesus is inextricably linked to seeking God's kingdom and the justice of that kingdom. Simply distancing ourselves from the rat race, withdrawing from the self-centeredness of the world, is not enough to bring freedom from anxiety. It takes a trust in God that results in active engagement with God's world, so as to challenge injustice wherever we encounter it, to set us truly free.

We don't have to go halfway round the world to encounter injustice. Most of us encounter it on a regular basis—in the casual sexism that demeans women and their potential that we meet in our workplaces and churches; in the unjust practices of large retail companies where we buy our cheap clothes; in the food we eat that has been procured by our food industry in a way that disadvantages small farmers in poorer parts of the world, and in a hundred other ways. We can start to build justice into our lifestyles in simple but meaningful ways, buying fairly traded foodstuffs, objecting to the sexism we encounter, and choosing not to buy from companies we know are guilty of exploitative practices in the developing world.

We can go further—pick a cause—sex trafficking, modern-day slavery, unfair international trade rules, hunger, homelessness—and join with others to make our voice of protest be heard, to contribute financially to end unjust practices, perhaps to travel to show solidarity with those who are oppressed or marginalized. Jesus followers ought to be at the forefront of the struggle against injustice, whereas too often we've withdrawn into our little holy circles. We get the idea of "righteousness," but "justice" is too often not high on the agenda. And yet the Greek word Matthew uses on the lips of Jesus is most likely best translated as "justice."

Seek God's kingdom and the kingdom's justice—aligning our lives with this idea is the key to dealing with all our anxieties. Bob Dylan in his "Theme Time Radio" show gave his listeners a short lesson on overcoming what he called the "holiday blues." It was a Christmas show, but no matter, what he said applies to any blues we might feel. "You don't need Dr. Phil . . . you don't need me," he said. "Just go out and help someone more unfortunate than you." In his own laconic drawl, Dylan suggested his listeners go to "a soup kitchen, or a retirement home, maybe even a prison" to find someone to be with and to bring some cheer to. "No matter how bad you have it, somebody got it worse. Instead of adding to the sadness in the world, why not help somebody out?"

Dylan's got it bang on. Turning outward to meet the need and the injustice in the world is the way to beat the blues, to beat a worried mind, no matter who we are, no matter what the nature of our anxiety is. As Willie Johnson said, if we take "Jesus's yoke upon us and live a Christian life," then "trouble will soon be over."

Listening Guide

Blind Blake, *The Best of,* Yazoo, 2000

Mose Allison, *Greatest Hits*, Decca, 2006

Blind Lemon Jefferson, *Black Snake Moan,* Complete Blues, 2008

Chris Thomas King, *The Soul of . . . ,* 21st Century Blues, 2003

ten

Preachin' the Blues

The Blues Are Black

Recently I watched Steve McQueen's movie *12 Years A Slave*, which tells the true story of a free African American, Solomon Northup, who lived in New York, but was kidnapped and sold into slavery in 1841. Northup ended up working in brutal conditions in Louisiana for twelve years before eventually being rescued and returned to his home and family in the North. The film, based on Northup's own book, depicts antebellum slavery in all its dehumanizing and barbarous reality. In one scene we see the slaves picking cotton, with the overseer cracking the whip. A song begins to rise from the pickers, led by one and answered by the others. It is at once plaintive and beautiful, unbearably sad and yet somehow an assertion of the slaves' humanity. And it is bluesy.

As I watched that scene, with all the other suffering, pain, and injustice that the film portrays running around in my head, I realized in a fresh way that I was watching the birth of the blues. McQueen's film, perhaps more than any before, tells the truth about slavery and the dark stain it has made on American history. And it is here in these sorrow songs, in these laments for all that has been lost, in these expressions of humanity in the face of oppression, that the blues emerged. No matter how expert white men and women become in playing the musical forms of the blues, essentially and originally, the blues are black.

As we've explored various sayings of Jesus in the Sermon on the Mount, we've discovered afresh something of the terrible injustice and suffering of black communities in the Southern states. We've seen the emergence of a new form of slavery that took place after Reconstruction and lasted until 1945, keeping black men in particular in bondage, working them to death in the mining and timber industries, and on farms. We've looked at the threat of being lynched, followed by hanging and/or burning on trumped-up charges. We've seen the conspiracy between the police, the judiciary, and business, which used the threat of violence, imprisonment, or neoslavery to terrorize black communities and exploit them for economic gain.

In the midst of all of this, the blues emerged and developed, giving a voice to the cry of pain and outrage from black people and as a means of asserting their human dignity. Even though the majority of blues songs are focused on romantic relationships, it is not difficult, knowing something of the historical context, to hear the reverberations of complaint about the experience of being black in the American South. But, as we have seen, there are many blues songs that explicitly protest the Jim Crow experience of blacks and many that implicitly refer to the horrors of lynching and white violence, where it was clearly too dangerous to be explicit.

The blues, then, is at once laments, cries for justice, howls of protest, and songs of hope for a better future. That being the case, as we suggested at the beginning of our journey, the blues is a fertile ground for reflecting on the gospel of Jesus Christ, given the important roles that lament, justice, protest, and hope play in it.

Crucial to our study is the notion that what Matthew has recorded for us of Jesus's teaching in the Sermon might actually be the gospel. Many Christians can't talk about the gospel without recourse to the writings of St. Paul. The idea of individual "justification by faith," which Paul explores in his letters to the churches in Galatia and Rome, has become so central for some modern Christians that it has *become* the gospel. This is not to deny the importance of what Paul has to say about God justifying or putting individuals right on the basis of the life, death, and resurrection of Jesus the Messiah, but the good news that Jesus came to announce is not wholly described by this idea.

There is, however, no disjoint between the good news preached by Jesus and the gospel preached by Paul. In answer to the question we posed at the beginning—"did Jesus preach the gospel?"—the answer is a resounding yes, but not on the contrived basis that he preached justification by faith. The answer is in the affirmative, in that both Jesus and Paul preached the good news that God's rule—his kingdom, government—had broken into our world and that the blessings of his peaceful reign, long hoped for and expected in Israel's scriptures, were beginning to break through.

The essence of the gospel—the good news—as the Prophet Isaiah had proclaimed, was "God reigns," and that the advent of God's reign would bring shalom and salvation. What we have in the Sermon is Jesus telling his followers what it is like to live as citizens of this new kingdom. It entailed a whole new way of life that anticipated the final day of renewal when the fullness of the kingdom would be evident, and that was quite contrary to the normal way of things in the world. The gospel, then, is about "justification," in the sense that it is about God putting things to rights—individuals, for sure, but also the whole world and the way the world works.

Justice and the Gospel

At the very heart of all this is the idea of justice. If justice revolves around the idea of setting things right, then this is at the very heart of the gospel. God's love and justice are not opposing ideas. God executes justice precisely because of God's love. As we have explored the biblical story, we have seen how God's intention has been to fix his broken world and that the means to do this was through the people he had chosen, Israel. Time and time again in the biblical narrative we get glimpses of Israel's understanding of her calling and we see the theme of justice threaded through the Old Testament, with provision in Israel's law for the weak and helpless, and in the prophetic critique of systems of oppression of the marginalized and poor.

Alongside this we have a continual cry, a lament for the way the world is, a howl of pain addressed to God about the suffering of his people, about the injustice they endure. The theme of brokenness, injustice, and the apparent triumph of evil resounds strongly through Israel's scriptures. The prophets sound this note of lament, bewailing both the unfaithfulness of God's people and the cruelty of her enemies.

As well as that long, loud lament, though, there comes a startling note of hope. Hope that God would break into history in a decisive way and put everything to rights—would bring justice once more to God's world. The way in which God did this, of course, was in the most surprising of ways—through Israel, as God had planned, but actually through one faithful Israelite, Jesus the Messiah. And furthermore, God's new day of renewal has come, not through confrontation and violence, but rather through the torture, execution, and subsequent resurrection of an innocent man.

Jesus's life and death proclaim loudly the nature of God's new kingdom, which has broken into the world. It is a kingdom of love, of peace, of compassion, of justice. His death and resurrection were both the means of God dealing with the problem of sin in God's world and a victory over evil. Jesus followers, through the Spirit, are empowered to form communities that experience within them the reality of the new kingdom, and demonstrate the upside-down values of this kingdom, which include humility, compassion, love, justice-seeking, and peacemaking, as well as joy and hope.

All this we have seen Jesus talk about in his Sermon, where he gives his followers a sense of the radical way in which they are to live, so as to testify to the reality of God's inbreaking new world.

The context in which the blues emerged and flourished reflects much of the experience of the people who lived in Israel in Old Testament times and of the very first Christians. They were largely poor and at times oppressed, suffering injustices from those around them. It is not surprising, then, that the blues reflect many of the concerns that we find in the biblical writers. We've looked at songs that reflect poverty, ill health, false imprisonment, betrayal, and social injustice. We've begun to hear the blues as a lament, a stark means of truth-telling about the state of the world and the oppression of a people. All this we find in our Bibles as well, especially in the Psalms and the Prophets. The blues are a reflection of the broken nature of our world and grab our attention with their straight-talking lyrics and haunting melodies. In a world where the media and advertising industries try to focus our attention on self-realization and the acquisition of stuff that we don't need, the blues' truth-telling snaps us out of our "modern daze," helping us realize that there is more going on in the world than our own self-satisfaction. The blues remind us that all around us, people are suffering, in desperate need of justice. In a world dominated by the gods of comfort and convenience, the blues calls our attention to the great sea of need all around us that cries out for our attention and engagement.

The reaction that we find in the blues to the injustices suffered by African Americans reminds us also of our complicity in injustice. It remains an open question as to whether white America has ever really come to terms with the realities of slavery, peonage, and Jim Crow discrimination and oppression. Today, the average black man in the US earns 30 percent less than his white counterpart, has a life expectancy of nearly four years less, is more likely to be living in poverty (27 percent of blacks were judged to be living in poverty against 10 percent of whites), and is incarcerated at nearly six times the rate of whites.[1]

Blues music is undeniably black, a crucial cultural expression rooted in black social history. That doesn't mean that the blues are closed to white people, either to listen to, dance to, or to play. What it does mean, however, is that white people need to listen to what the blues tell us about our own history and the ways in which our group may have been involved in the oppression of previous generations. Clearly this is not just something that is relevant to white Americans—many of us live in regions where the repercussions of previous years of discrimination or oppression are still felt today. The blues should alert us to injustices in our own history. By telling the truth about what went on, the blues highlight the need to understand our own present in the light of the past and to ensure that every vestige of discrimination is rooted out.

Justice, Women, and the Blues

One area where this is important is with respect to women. You don't have to listen to the blues for very long to be struck by some of the sexist, indeed misogynist lyrics. Robert Johnson, for example, sings about his "Kind-Hearted Woman," who will do anything for him—all very nice, until the last verse where he accuses her of studying evil all the time and wanting to kill him. "Terraplane Blues" uses the sexual metaphor of a car for a woman's body. Johnson asks the woman, "Who been drivin' my Terraplane for you?" while he's been away, seemingly considering this woman to be his property. It does get worse, of course, with Johnson's "32–20 Blues," where the singer says, "Little girl, little girl, I got mean things on my mind"—the sort of mean things, perhaps, that surface in "Me and the Devil Blues," where Johnson is "goin' to beat my woman until I get satisfied."

Blues music, like much else in popular culture over the past 100 years, has at times ignored women, objectified them, or vilified them. And in case you think that this is all so much ancient history, and that the feminist movement of the last fifty years has won the day, sexism and misogyny is rife in all sorts of expressions of popular culture, from national tabloid newspapers to rap and hip-hop lyrics and videos, to heavy metal music, to the film, fashion, and beauty industries.

1. US Current Population Survey and the National Committee on Pay Equity; US Centers for Disease Control and Prevention; www.naacp.org

Throughout the world women are facing a virtual tsunami of violence. Domestic violence, rape, and sexual assaults against women still occur with shocking frequency—staggeringly, it is reckoned that one in three women on the planet will be beaten or raped during her lifetime.

The charity Oxfam recently said "From London to Lahore, inequality between men and women persists." This is not just true in war-torn African countries where women suffer rape and violence, or in Islamic countries like Saudi Arabia where women are not allowed to drive, vote, or participate in sport and suffer patriarchy in virtually every aspect of their lives, or in India where female abortion is still rife—it's true in advanced Western societies in Europe and in the US. In the UK, official figures still show that women working full-time typically earn about 16 percent less than men.[2] The US is no better, with women typically earning 23 percent less than men. In politics, only 18 percent of the members of Congress are women and in an international ranking of the equality of men and women in parliaments, the UK comes in at sixty-fourth place, behind Tunisia and Zimbabwe.[3]

So what about the Christian church, then—where its first theologian, Paul, said that in Christ, there was no Jew or Gentile, no slave or free, and no male or female? Sadly, part of the history of the church has been a history of inequality for women—the church through the centuries has been blatantly androcentric and at times, misogynist. This despite the way the New Testament portrays women so positively in the ministry of Jesus and within the context of the early Christian communities. In Paul's letter to the Christians at Rome, he sends his greetings to the Roman house church leaders, a number of whom are clearly women, and one, Junia, whom he recognizes as an apostle—a senior Christian leader—and who he says was "outstanding" amongst the apostles. Despite various recent attempts to make Junia into a man (!) or to explain away her apostleship, the weight of evidence indicates we must side with the fourth-century theologian, Chrysostom, who said, "Even to be an apostle is great, but also to be prominent among them—consider how wonderful a song of honour that is. Glory be! How great the wisdom of this woman that she was even deemed worthy of the apostle's title."[4]

2. OECD Social Policy Division, 2010; Trade Unions Congress, 2013; and Smith, "The Gender Pay Gap," *Forbes*, 2013.

3. International Organization of Parliaments.

4. For an excellent treatment of the history of Junia in New Testament studies, see Epp, *Junia*.

In the early history of the blues, the biggest stars by far were the women artists like Mamie Smith, Bessie Smith, Ma Rainey, Victoria Spivey, and her cousin, Sippie Wallace. Ma Rainey was one of the first to record the blues in 1920 and she and the others went on to be big recording stars. Bessie Smith, the Empress of the Blues, recorded more than 160 songs and with her big voice, big personality, and sensational outfits, filled venues wherever she performed, including theatres in New York's Harlem. And of course the history of women in the blues continues to this day with great artists like Etta James, Irma Thomas, Bonnie Raitt, Susan Tedeschi, Mavis Staples, Carolyn Wonderland, Grace Potter, Shemekia Copeland—the list is a long one.

The checkered history of women and attitudes to women in the blues alerts us to the question of the church's own history with respect to women. The resistance that, sadly, is still around in some quarters to the clear evidence in the New Testament of women in church leadership—like Junia, Phoebe, and Prisca—combined with the casual sexism found in many congregations, and the persistence of gender-specific and woman-excluding language in worship, hymns, and Bible translations, is to be regretted. In addition, given the current levels of violence against women in both Western and developing-world societies, Jesus followers need to be much more aware of the issue of justice—and thus of the gospel—that is at stake here and need to be in the vanguard of those seeking to liberate women from sex slavery, domestic violence, female genital mutilation, and all forms of discrimination.

The Blues, the Gospel, and Peace

A key component of the renewed world that is emerging through the life, death, and resurrection of Jesus is the idea of shalom or peace. This Jewish idea is a broad one that refers to human flourishing. It is not simply the absence of war, but it certainly includes that. Wars around our world today create the most terrible human suffering, particularly for innocent non-combatants who become subject to maiming, homelessness, disease, hunger, rape, and violent death. "Clinical strikes" against only military targets by aerial drones and the like do not exist. War inflicts immense suffering on innocent women, children, and men in the first instance.

Despite the admonitions of Jesus to "love your enemies" and to feel blessed when persecuted, many Christians have made peace with war.

Patriotism trumps loyalty to the new kingdom of God, calling into question the very nature of the faith of these "Christians." A commitment to "our way of life," to protecting at all costs our economic prosperity, is somehow contrived to be able to sit alongside faith in Jesus. Yet the God of the New Testament is the "God of peace," and Jesus is the "prince of peace." Many Christians are far too ready to go to war—when actually, our first responsibility, according to Jesus in the Sermon, is to love and pray for our enemies. As blueswoman Carolyn Wonderland says in "Only God Knows When": "Violence is no solution when life doesn't suit your plans."

The blues remind us of the lack of shalom, or human flourishing, that exists throughout the world because of war, corruption, unjust trading rules, climate change, and a hundred other reasons. Just as black communities suffered from the lack of shalom during the Jim Crow era, so too do many communities throughout the world, particularly in the developing world. For them, as for Little Brother Montgomery, a barrelhouse blues pianist, the blues "be's with me every morning, Lord, and every night and noon." Or as Robert Johnson put it, the blues were "fallin' down like hail, And the day keeps on worryin' me."

The world's poor have "worried minds"—their uncertain existence makes them anxious about a great many things. The gospel of Jesus Christ, the gospel of peace, is only good news in so far as we demonstrate that good news to a needy world. Turning our backs on war is only a start—we are to anticipate the shalom-ful, compassionate, just kingdom of God through our lives as individuals and communities of Jesus followers. Humanitarians like Bill Gates have begun to show that disease and poverty can be dealt with in the world, if there is a will. Those of us who claim to follow the God of peace need to find ways of being in the forefront of tackling the major problems in the world in a way that demonstrates both the justice and love of God.

Surprisingly, those of us who are relatively well-off, in global terms, somehow contrive to have anxious minds as well. Our worries, however, often revolve around not needs, but wants. Conditioned by our consumerist economy, we let our attention become diverted away from the real needs of the world to our supposed needs. Like Solomon we have become consumed by acquisitiveness and vanity—an attitude that Jesus warns against in the Sermon, exhorting us to seek God's kingdom and to trust God for our needs as we do so. It is as we turn away from our own anxious self-seeking to serve the needs of others that we will find true freedom from a "worried mind."

The Blues, the Gospel, and a Better World

As well as alerting us to the pain and sorrow in the world, the blues, counterintuitively, sounds a note of hope. As it was sung and danced to in juke joints on the weekends, it was a means of African Americans asserting their humanity, which all week long had been denied by the Jim Crow society in which they sought to make their way.

Somehow, in the midst of the worried mind and the troubles of the blues, it often manage to hit a note of hope. B. B. King, carrying the hopes of his people, sang "There must be a better world somewhere." This idea and aspiration is, as we have seen, integral to the gospel of Jesus Christ. Tom Wright's comment is worth noting again, "To hope for a better future in this world—for the poor, the sick, the lonely and depressed, for the slaves, the refugees, the hungry and homeless, for the abused, the paranoid, the downtrodden and despairing, and in fact for the whole wide, wonderful and wounded world—is not something else, something extra, something tacked on to 'the gospel' as an afterthought."[5]

At the heart of the gospel is the idea of God fixing God's world—it is not about taking believers off to some set of luxury apartments in the sky. Clearly that includes, quite fundamentally, fixing broken people. The blues, while they speak to us of the suffering and injustice of a people, also present us with individuals whose lives need to be healed and restored. They include bluesmen and women who have lost their way in rambling and addictions; ordinary people suffering the result of their own or others' selfishness; women and men who are themselves violent and out of control. To these and all the rest of the broken, sinning, wayward ones in the world, Jesus in the Sermon offers forgiveness and the opportunity of getting on to the "road that leads to life" (Matt 7:14). There is hope for all, there are new possibilities for change and transformation for everyone who is prepared to follow Jesus along this "hard" road.

For those of us who are his disciples, Jesus has taught us to pray that things would be done God's way—bringing peace, love, and justice—here on earth, just as they are in God's realm. Jesus followers need to take this hope seriously and to begin anticipating God's new world by the way that

5. Wright, *Surprised by Hope*, 204.

we live here and now. As the blues have taught us, we need to lament for the state of the world; we need to recognize the injustice that gives rise to "worried minds"; but we also need to both keep our eyes on the hope of God's new future for the world and to be part of God's answers to the problems we see around us. And, in addition to that, as Luther Dickinson and Johnny Cash have reminded us, there is a hope beyond this life, the assurance that Jesus followers will share in the full reality of God's transformed world— "ain't no grave can hold this body down."

We started out with Stephen Nichols's question in mind—what does Jerusalem have to do with the Delta? The answer, it seems, is rather a lot. The blues, as an art form forged in adversity and suffering, becomes an appropriate point of departure for considering matters of faith and a gospel which itself was forged in the suffering of the innocent. If we let it, the blues can help us reach deep into our faith and understand the world, ourselves, and the gospel that little bit better.

Bibliography

Ames, R. *The Story of American Folk Song*. New York: Grosset & Dunlap, 1960.

Augustus. *Res Gestae Divi Augusti*. Translated by Frederick W. Shipley. Cambridge, MA: Harvard University Press, 1924.

Bane, Michael. *White Boy Singing the Blues*. London: Penguin, 1982.

Bauckham, Richard. *God Crucified*. Grand Rapids: Eerdmans, 1998.

Best, Ernest. *Ephesians*. Edinburgh: T & T Clark, 1998.

Beaumont, Daniel. *Preachin' the Blues: The Life & Times of Son House*. Oxford: Oxford University Press, 2011.

Blackmon, D. A. *Slavery by Another Name: The Re-Enslavement of Black Americans from the Civil War to World War II*. London: Icon, 2012.

Botkin, B. A. *Lay My Burden Down: A Folk History of Slavery*. Chicago: University of Chicago Press, 1972.

Brueggemann, Walter. *Disruptive Grace*. London: SCM, 2011.

———. *Theology of the Old Testament*. Minneapolis: Fortress, 1997.

———. *Truth Speaks to Power: The Countercultural Nature of Scripture*. Louisville: Westminster John Knox, 2013.

Calt, S., and G. Wardlow. *King of the Delta Blues: The Life and Music of Charlie Patton*. Newton, NJ: Rock Chapel, 1991.

Carter, Warren. *Matthew and the Margins: A Sociopolitical and Religious Reading*. JSNTS 204. Sheffield: Sheffield Academic, 2000.

———. *The Roman Empire and the New Testament: An Essential Guide*. Nashville: Abingdon, 2006.

Charters, S. *The Poetry of the Blues*. New York: Avon, 1963.

Cicero, *De re publica*. Translated by Clinton Walker Keyes. London: Heinemann, 1928.

Clinton, C. *Harriet Tubman: the Road to Freedom*. New York: Little, Brown & Co., 2004.

Clinton, Hillary. *Living History*. London: Headline, 2004.

Clinton, William. "Statement by President Clinton on the Passing of Nelson Mandela." Clinton Foundation. http://www.clintonfoundation.org/press-releases/statement-president-clinton-passing-nelson-mandela.

Cone, James H. *The Cross and the Lynching Tree*. Maryknoll, NY: Orbis, 2011.

———. *The Spirituals and the Blues*. Maryknoll, NY: Orbis, 1991.

Conetta, Carl. "Operation Eduring Freedom: Why a Higher Rate of Civilian Bombing Casualties." Project on Defense Alternatives Briefing Report 13. http://www.comw.org/pda/02010ef.html.

Crossan, Dominic. *The Historical Jesus: The Life of a Mediterranean Jewish Peasant*. San Francisco: Harper Collins, 1991.

Davids, H. "New Testament Foundations for Living More Simply." In *Living More Simply,* edited by Ronald J. Sider, 40–58. London: Hodder & Stoughton, 1982.

Desmond Tutu Peace Foundation. http://www.tutufoundationusa.org/welcome-to-the-dtpf-peacemaker-toolkit/peace-being-a-peacemaker-topic-page/peace-can-you-visualize-it/.

Desmond Tutu Foundation UK Facebook post, September 21, 2012. http://www.facebock.com/TutuFoundationUK/posts/464624380227289.

Dixon, Willie, with Don Snowden. *I Am the Blues: The Willie Dixon Story.* New York: Da Capo, 1989.

Douglass, Frederick. "My Bondage and My Freedom." In *Readings in Black American Music,* edited by E. Southern, 82–87. New York: Norton, 1971.

Du Bois, W. E. B. *The American Negro, His History and Literature.* Cambridge, MA: MIT Press, 1970.

———. "Ida B. Wells-Barnett: Postscript." *The Crisis,* June 1931, 207.

———. *The Souls of Black Folk.* 1903. New York: Fawcett, 1961.

Eareckson Tada, Joni. *A Place of Healing: Wrestling with the Mysteries of Suffering, Pain, and God's Sovereignty.* Colorado Springs: D. C. Cook, 2010.

Edwards, D., et al. *The World Don't Owe Me Nothing.* Chicago: Chicago Review, 1997.

Epp, Eldon Jay. *Junia: The First Woman Apostle.* Minneapolis: Fortress, 2005.

Clapton, Eric, interviewed by Bob Edwards. "Eric Clapton Takes on Robert Johnson's Blues." *Morning Edition,* March 30, 2004. http://www.npr.org/templates/story/story.php?storyId=1798862.

France, R. T. *The Gospel of Matthew.* Grand Rapids: Eerdmans, 2007.

Galishoff, S. "Germs Know No Color Line: Black Health and Public Policy in Atlanta, 1900–1918." *Journal of the History of Medicine* 40 (January 1985) 22–41.

Garon, P. *Blues and the Poetic Spirit.* New York: Da Capo, 1978.

Garon, P., and B. Garon. *Woman with Guitar: Memphis Minnie's Blues.* New York: Da Capo, 1992.

Gilmour, Michael J. *Gods And Guitars: Seeking the Sacred in Post-1960s Popular Music.* Waco, TX: Baylor University Press, 2009.

Giola, Ted. *Delta Blues.* New York: Norton, 2008.

Gonzalez, Antonio. *God's Reign and the End of Empires.* Miami: Convivium, 2012.

Gussow, Adam. *Seems Like Murder Here: Southern Violence and the Blues Tradition.* Chicago: University of Chicago, 2002.

Hagner, Donald A. *Matthew 1–13: Word Biblical Commentary.* Dallas: Word, 1993.

Handy, W. C. *Father of the Blues: An Autobiography.* 1941. New York: Da Capo, 1991.

Hays, Richard. *The Moral Vision of the New Testament.* Edinburgh: T & T Clark, 1996.

International Organization of Parliaments. http://www.ipu.org/wmn-e/classif.htm.

Jewett, Robert. *Romans.* Minneapolis: Fortress, 2007.

Julian. *The Works of the Emperor Julian.* Translated by Wilmer Cave Wright. Cambridge, MA: Harvard University Press, 1913–1923.

King, B. B. *Blues All Around Me.* New York: HarperCollins, 1996.

King, Martin Luther, Jr. *I Have a Dream: Writings and Speeches That Changed the World.* Edited by J. M. Washington. New York: HarperCollins, 1992.

King, Martin Luther, Sr., with C. Riley. *Daddy King: An Autobiography.* New York: William Morrow & Co., 1980.

Kirk, J. R. Daniel. *Jesus Have I Loved, but Paul?* Grand Rapids: Baker, 2011.

Knox, John. *Chapters in a Life of Paul.* Rev. ed. London: SCM, 1989.

Kornbluth, Jesse. "Johnny Cash's 'Ain't No Grave': Did 250,000 Volunteer Artists in 17 Countries Make 2010's Best Video?" *Huffington Post*, November 9, 2010. http://www.huffingtonpost.com/jesse-kornbluth/john-cashs-aint-no-grave_b_780975.html).

Kraybill, Donald. *The Upside Down Kingdom*. Harrisonburg, VA: Herald, 2003.

Lester, Julius. "I Can Make My Own Songs: An Interview With Son House." *Sing Out!*, vol. 15, no. 3 (July 1965) 38–47.

Lewis, C. S. *The Screwtape Letters*. New York: HarperOne, 2009.

Litwack, Leon F. *Trouble in Mind: Black Southerners in the Age of Jim Crow*. New York: Vintage, 1999.

Longenecker, Bruce W. *Remember the Poor: Paul, Poverty and the Greco-Roman World*. Grand Rapids: Eerdmans, 2010.

Maffly-Kipp, Laurie F. "An Introduction to the Church in the Southern Black Community," May 2001. http://docsouth.unc.edu/church/intro.html.

Mandela, Nelson. *Long Walk to Freedom: The Autobiography*. Boston: Little, Brown, 1994.

Mauser, U. *The Gospel of Peace*. Louisville: Westminster John Knox, 1992.

Mays, Benjamin E. *Born to Rebel: An Autobiography*. New York: Scribner, 1971.

Meggitt, J. *Paul, Poverty and Survival*. Edinburgh: T & T Clark, 1998.

McKnight, Scot. *The King Jesus Gospel*. Grand Rapids: Zondervan, 2011.

Murray, Albert. *Stomping the Blues*. New York: McGraw-Hill, 1976.

Murray, P. *Proud Shoes: The Story of an American Family*. New York: Harper, 1956.

Nardoni, Enrique. *Rise Up, O Judge: A Study of Justice in the Biblical World*. Peabody, MA: Hendrickson, 2004.

Nichols, Stephen J. *Getting the Blues*. Grand Rapids: Brazos, 2008.

Oakes, P. *Philippians: From People to Letter*. Cambridge: Cambridge University Press, 2007.

———. *Reading Romans in Pompeii: Paul's Letter at Ground Level*. London: SPCK 2009.

Oakley, G. *The Devil's Music: A History of the Blues*. 2nd ed. New York: Da Capo, 1997.

O'Connor, Kathleen. *Lamentations and the Tears of the World*. Maryknoll, NY: Orbis, 2002.

OECD Social Policy Division. "Gender Brief," 2010. http://www.oecd.org/els/family/44720649.pdf.

Oliver, Paul. *Conversations with the Blues*. New York: Cassell, 1965.

Palmer, R. *Deep Blues*. New York: Penguin, 1981.

Perkins, John M. *Let Justice Roll Down*. Ventura, CA: Regal, 1976.

Price, S. R. F. *Rituals and Power: The Roman Imperial Cult in Asia Minor*. Cambridge: Cambridge University Press, 1984.

Raper, A. F. *The Tragedy of Lynching*. Chapel Hill, NC: University of North Carolina Press, 1933.

Robinson, James H. *Road Without Turning: The Story of Reverend James H. Robinson: An Autobiography*. New York: Farrar, Straus & Giroux, 1950.

Rosner, Brian S. *Greed as Idolatry: The Origins and Meaning of a Pauline Metaphor*. Grand Rapids: Eerdmans, 2007.

Scharen, Christian. *Broken Hallelujahs*. Grand Rapids: Brazos, 2011.

Scheper-Hughes, Nancy, and Philippe I. Bourgois. *Violence in War and Peace*. Malden, MA: Blackwell, 2003.

Scorsese, Martin, director. *Feel Like Going Home*. Vulcan/Reverse Angle International, 2003.

Shaw, A. *The World of the Soul*. New York: Coronet Communications, 1971.

Smith, Kyle. "The Gender Pay Gap." *Forbes*, 2013. http://www.forbes.com/sites/kylesmith/2014/04/10/the-gender-pay-gap-is-just-the-beginning-of-americas-pay-inequity-problem/.

Sobrino, Jon. *No Salvation Outside the Poor: Prophetic-Utopian Essays*. Maryknoll, NY: Orbis, 2008.

Steele, Jonathan. "Forgotten Victims." *The Guardian*, May 20, 2002.

Stockman, Steve. *The Rock Cries Out*. Lake Mary, FL: Relevant, 2004.

Storkey, Alan. *Jesus and Politics: Confronting the Powers*. Grand Rapids: Baker, 2005.

Swartley, Willard M. *Covenant of Peace: The Missing Peace in New Testament Theology and Ethics*. Grand Rapids: Eerdmans, 2006.

Tacitus. *The Annals of Tacitus*. Translated by A. J. Church and W. J. Brodribb. London: Macmillan, 1877.

Tooze, Sandra B. *Muddy Waters: the Mojo Man*. Toronto: ECW, 1997.

Trade Unions Congress, 2013. http://ww.tuc.org.uk/equality-issues/gender/equality/equal-pay/shock-rise-gender-pay-gap-after-years-slow-steady-progress.

Tuff, Antoinette. Interview with ABC News, August 20, 2013. http://abcnews.go.com/Us/elementary-school-clerk-convinced-suspect-put-weapons-surrender/story?id=20014879&singlePage=true.

———. Interview with *Forbes,* 2013. http://www.forbes.com/sites/85broads/2013/08/26/the-power-of-just-one-woman/.

Tutu, Desmond. *God Has a Dream*. New York: Doubleday, 2004.

Virgil. *The Aeneid*. Translated by J. W. Mackail. London: Macmillan, 1908.

Wardlow, G. D. *Chasin' That Devil Music: Searching for the Blues*. San Francisco: Backbeat, 1998.

Wells, Ida B. "Our Country's Lynching Record." In *Ida B. Wells-Barnett: An Exploratory Study of an American Black Woman, 1893–1930,* by M. I. Thompson, 277–79. Brooklyn, NY: Carlson, 1990.

Whalin, W. Terry. *Sojourner Truth: American Abolitionist*. Uhrichsville, OH: Barbour, Kindle Edition, 2013.

World Bank. "Data on Poverty and Inequality." http:web.worldbank.org.

Wilson, A. N. *The Mind of Paul the Apostle*. London: Sinclair-Stevenson, 1998.

Wink, Walter. *The Powers that Be: Theology for a New Millennium*. New York: Harmony, 1998.

———. *Unmasking the Powers*. Philadelphia: Fortress, 1986.

Winter, Bruce W. *Seek the Welfare of the City: Christians as Benefactors and Citizens*. Grand Rapids: Eerdmans, 1994.

Wolkin, J. M., and B. Keenom. *Michael Bloomfield: If You Love These Blues*. San Francisco: Backbeat, 2000.

Wolterstorff, Nicholas. *Justice: Rights and Wrongs*. Princeton, NJ: Princeton University, 2008.

Wright, N. T. *The Climax of the Covenant*. Edinburgh: T & T Clark, 1991.

———. *Evil and the Justice of God*. Downers Grove, IL: InterVarsity, 2006.

———. *Jesus and the Victory of God*. London: SPCK, 1996.

———. *The New Testament and the People of God*. London: SPCK, 1992.

———. *Paul for Everyone: Galatians and Thessalonians*. London: SCM, 2002.

———. *Paul in Fresh Perspective*. Minneapolis: Fortress, 2005.

———. "Paul's Gospel and Caesar's Empire." In *Paul and Politics,* edited by Richard A. Horsley, 160–83. Harrisburg: Trinity Press, 2000.

————. *Surprised by Hope.* London: SPCK, 2011.

————. *When God Became King.* London: SPCK, 2011.

Wright, Richard. "Black Boy (American Hunger)." In Richard Wright, *Later Works,* 1–365. New York: Library of America, 1991.

Yoder Neufeld, Thomas. "For he is our peace: Ephesians 2:11–22." In *Beautiful Upon the Mountains,* edited by M. Shertz and H. Friesen, 215–34. Scottdale, PA: Herald, 2004.

Lightning Source UK Ltd.
Milton Keynes UK
UKOW05f0357191214

243381UK00001B/2/P